ABOUT THE AUTHORS

Lola Olufemi is a black feminist and organiser from London. She graduated from Cambridge with a degree in English Literature in 2016. She facilitated FLY, the group for women and non-binary people of colour at Cambridge from 2015-16 and held roles on the BME and Women's Campaign. She was the Cambridge University Students Union Women's Officer from 2017-18. During her time at university she was heavily involved in student activism, working on, amongst others: the establishment of support for survivors of sexual violence, decolonising the curriculum and opposing the marketisation of higher education. She is currently the NUS Second Place on the NUS Women's Campaign & sits on the National Executive Council. She is a masters student in Gender Studies who is interested in black feminist thought as a vehicle for thinking about the self and others and disrupting systems of power. She is currently writing a book on reclaiming feminism for young people which will be published by Pluto Press in 2020.

Odelia Younge is an educator and writer based in Oakland, California. In her life and work, she centers discussions about blackness and resistance. Odelia earned a B.A. in history and literature from Harvard and an MPhil in politics, development and democratic education from Cambridge. Her research has focused on black women collectives, historical memory, transgressions and resistance, and black male youth identity within spatial theory, critical youth studies, and radical black feminist theory. Odelia also has a background in peace education and children's rights, developing programs in places such as Miami, Florida and the Greater Accra region of Ghana. She has led work across the United States on transforming education, decolonising systems, and building out spaces for black writers, while also organizing spaces for creative expression. Odelia is driven by her faith, radical black love, and the concept of creating yourself to freedom -- forgetting what your oppressors have told you is the truth, and building anew. Odelia is the co-founder of Novalia Collective, which focuses on storytelling, community building, and cultivating spaces that vanquish fear of uncertainty and the unknown.

Waithera Sebatindira is a Law graduate from Trinity Hall and recently completed her MPhil in Multi-disciplinary Gender Studies at the same College. While facilitator of FLY, and with the indispensable support of its founders and a group of committed women of colour, she expanded the group's membership and reach. During this time, Waithera developed a black feminist ethic that continues to be informed by the work of inspirational women she reads and meets – especially this book's co-authors. She went on to become the first woman of colour to hold the position of full-time Women's Officer on the Cambridge University Students' Union and, during her tenure, campaigned on behalf of woman and non-binary students on campus while coordinating decolonial efforts across campus.

Suhaiymah Manzoor-Khan is a writer, spoken-word poet, and educator invested in unlearning the modalities of knowledge she has internalised, disrupting power relations, and asking questions around narratives to do with race, gender, Islamophobia, state violence and decoloniality. She did her BA in History at Queens' College, Cambridge, and MA in Postcolonial Studies at SOAS. Alongside a wider education from the epistemology of Islam and work of women of colour and anti-systemic thinkers from across the world, Suhaiymah regularly speaks and workshops on racism, Islamophobia, feminism and poetry across the UK as well as writing about those topics at her website, www.thebrownhijabi.com. Her work has been featured in The Independent, The Guardian, Al-Jazeera, BBC, The Islam Channel, ITV, Sky TV, TEDx conferences, music festivals, US slams and British Universities. She is trying her best to destabilise accepted narratives and disrupt the tendency to fall into binary explanations, insha'Allah.

Jun Pang is a writer and perpetual student, based between Hong Kong and the UK. She co-founded and edits daikon*, a creative platform for South-East and East Asian non-binary people and women in Europe.

A FLY Girl's Guide to University:
Being a Woman of Colour at Cambridge and Other Institutions of Power and Elitism

Lola Olufemi, Odelia Younge, Waithera Sebatindira and Suhaiymah Manzoor-Khan

Featuring poems by Jun Pang
Compiled and Edited by Odelia Younge

VERVE
POETRY PRESS
BIRMINGHAM

PUBLISHED BY VERVE POETRY PRESS
Birmingham, West Midlands, UK
https://vervepoetrypress.com
mail@vervepoetrypress.com

FIRST PUBLISHED JAN 2019

REPRINTED FEB 2019 / OCT 2019

Printed and bound in the UK by Imprint Digital

ISBN: 978-1-912565-14-6

Cover Art Design by Sheena Zhang

*For every woman of colour who they will attempt to
contain and conquer. They can't.*

*For every 'unacceptable' person who causes discomfort
simply by existing in places they were not meant to.
Keep going, you are not alone.*

*For the voices always told to quiet down.
Seek ways to yell.*

*For the ancestors, for every one of us, and all of
those yet to come.*

NOTE FROM THE EDITOR

"I am slightly concerned... the market is so tricky and placing a book of this kind is not always easy... if you ever write a fiction book that would of course be a different matter – and if you do, please send it to me!"

Those were the words from a publishing company that we sent our book manuscript to after it was completed.

Wouldn't it be nice to read a book about the experiences of four women of colour and at the end be able to say 'thank goodness that wasn't real'? That women of colour's lives, our stories, are best digested by others as works of our imagination.

So we set it aside. Not because we didn't believe in the importance of this book, but simply because life kept happening, and there was no time to convince publishing houses of the worth of women of colour's words, when we were busy doing the work out in the world. And now it's been three years.

Returning to these pieces three years later as editor and compiler, combing through each piece with new insight, I am aware of how much has changed, yet I remain, as always, deeply proud of this work. Not because it is a perfect encapsulation of who we are in the present, but because I am committed to growth, not just in myself, but in others as well. We must invest in a constant commitment to do better once we know better; to speak more life, once we know what death looks like. Alicia Garza, one of the co-founders of Black Lives Matter:

*"I remember who I was before I gave my life to the movement. Someone was patient with me. Someone saw that I had something to contribute. Someone stuck with me. Someone did the work to increase my commitment. Someone taught me how to be accountable. Someone opened my eyes to the root causes of the problems we face. Someone pushed me to call forward my vision for the future. Someone trained me to bring other people who are looking for a movement into one."**

It's easy to see all the things we aren't, to get anxious that there is so much to learn and become, and to get impatient with everything that happens in the middle. But we wrote this nonetheless because the time is always now to speak your truth. Our 'someones' that Garza spoke about were the other members of FLY and many other women of colour in our lives.

Everything we have written here were our truths, and everything we have written here has also been understood in new ways as we continue to change and to grow. My feeling that this book should exist has only intensified over these years, with each word of this book I have read and reread. I'm glad life took us back to these pages so that others, too, could find them.

-Odelia.

---

* Garza, Alicia. *"Our cynicism will not build a movement. Collaboration will."* Mic. 2017

CONTENTS

FOREWORD

You need to see yourself reflected in images of success to believe that they are possible.

At age fourteen, I made it onto a "gifted and talented" school trip to Cambridge University because someone dropped out. Weaving through the many 31 Colleges of the University, I tallied every black person I saw. At an ancient institution, historically a finishing school for the white male elite, I needed to know if I could imagine myself within its sandstone structures, populated by faces that didn't look like my own.

Six years on, as Black schoolgirls point to a friend and me on the King's Parade and shout "eight, nine!" it struck me instantly that they were doing the same as I had years back. Despite the brief nature of the encounter, I still wonder if the mere sight of us, two Black women— *students* at the University of Cambridge—, might have coloured a white-washed expectation, or shifted their imaginings of a future at Cambridge

I believe that this is the inherent power of visibility: it uncovers what might be possible in the face of what first appears structurally impossible.

The University of Cambridge is a total of its 31 Colleges, 7 academic Schools and many other parts. Within four weeks of my first term at Girton College, I realised just what that meant for the ability of BME[1] students to reach out to one another and form part of a larger whole. At any one College, like my own, you could be one of two or three black students in your year, or College overall. In my College, I was one of four. That is, until the two exchange students returned to MIT[2] to finish their degrees back home.

The realisation that the departure of two students could cut the Black representation within my institution by fifty percent struck me; I was not sure I could exist at an institution where my first and foremost descriptor might be "*the* Black girl". FLY was born of that desire for an alternative descriptor. FLY took root because women of colour studying at Cambridge decided we wanted to 'speak as women, because we are women, and do not need others to speak for us.'

I met Precious, my best friend, through FLY. Initially five black women in the Cambridge Waterstones Cafe, I think we did, in fact, believe that we were creating something momentous and worthwhile, something that could affirm black womanhood through conversations about race, gender and class. As the support system throughout my degree, FLY was and is a gift of political energy, love, motivation and sisterhood. Three years on, I am the first Black woman to be President of the Cambridge University Students' Union, and I watch the collective voice and action of FLY Girls change the face of our institution, enriching the ancient hallways with every meeting and event. FLY demands that the existence and contributions of BME women in the academy be genuinely acknowledged and included at Cambridge, without superficial compromises.

As a working class, first generation Black British African woman, the University of Cambridge opened up a vast world of people, ideas and value systems. It also showed me the deep running flaws of our world, which pivot on inequality and its subsequent prejudices. Of course,

---

[1]BME stands for 'Black, Minority and Ethnic students. BME students organized from the terms used in the UK census.

[2]Massachusetts Institute of Technology; a university in Cambridge, Massachusetts in the U.S.

there were those moments during my studies where casual prejudices snatched away my sense of belonging, and I found myself craving a space free from some diffuse sense of expectation I believed I had to meet on behalf of all Black people and women, everywhere.

'FLY' means Freedom Loving You which could not be more fitting given the constraining nature of stereotypes that women of colour often confront in a bid to show they are politically or academically as capable as their white counterparts. Whether it is the proverbial "race card" when women of colour call out prejudice, or the "quota" jibe, which seeks to discredit our place in academia, women of colour have to collectivise and build their own platform on which they can be heard. I am honoured to have been part of this trailblazing collective of women who set down building blocks for minority women who will arrive at the halls of Cambridge for centuries to come.

It was Audre Lorde who stated 'Black feminists speak as women, because we are women and do not need others to speak for us.' The essays you will find here are just that. They belong to the women of colour who defy the sometimes latent, sometimes overt, prejudice and discrimination which seeks to polarise, mystify, or demean their lived experience and equal membership in this world.

Women of colour continue to fight for the complex nature of their existence to be rendered as equally valid, real and nuanced as their white counterparts. Thus, I no longer agonise over what might become of FLY when my time within the Cambridge bubble ends. I know that as this political, cultural and academic fight continues, so too will FLY.

Priscilla Mensah, FLY Co-Founder
Cambridge, Cambridgeshire, United Kingdom, July 2016

PREFACE

i will hold this space for your return.
i will hold this space because
everyone of your lives, is our life.
this poem is searching for
You.
You.
You.
....
this poem will find you.

– *chibol (the immutable measure of black life.)* nayyirah waheed

The words of nayyirah waheed sit with me as I reflect on the process of writing and editing this book with three other women of colour I am grateful to know. There is no amount of pages that exist that could capture the experiences we have all had in our lives. No concoction of phrases that could adequately describe the feelings and emotions that walk with us daily in the spaces we enter—whether because we are welcomed in them or not. It is through this writing, however, that I have found a language to share in that honours the spaces we create when we inhabit institutions like Cambridge. Living within, yet beyond, those spaces with the audacity to refuse their questioning of our existence. Whilst our backs bear the burdens that the world lays upon them, they are also the strength upon which we stand—alone and together.

The Oxbridge[3] experience has a face and a narrative attached to it. That face is often the main character in a story of white cisgender males that society has laid out a path to traditional positions of 'power.' It is a narrative embedded in systems of oppression and serves as the proof-point for the maintenance of old boys clubs. These institutions are aesthetically beautiful places, but surrounded by ugly walls of insulation—ivory towers that allow others to look in and maybe enter, but never to fully participate. But that is not a complete narrative.

There are those of us who find ourselves, for a multitude of reasons, on the other side of those walls, within the ivory towers. Our existence is acknowledged as 'progress', but only as long as we play the role in the narrative that is written for us: studious, quiet and grateful, without intent to rock the boat. But we do exist. We are here. There may not be many of us, but we are very much present. These institutions must be made aware of this, even if they don't expand their spaces for us. We do not seek equal representation to take part in systems of oppression, but rather the ability to freely create and become, without fear of obliteration.

In the summer of 2015 I began to reflect on my time at Cambridge as my studies came to an end. I was a graduate student who had found herself once more in the midst of a world shrouded in whiteness and its power and privilege. When I spoke to people about Cambridge, they too believed the narrative of the white, cisgender male who graduated atop the rest of the country, the world at his fingertips. When I shared stories of police harassment, marginalisation, and erasure, people either did not know whether to believe them as singular events, or they sympathised at a surface level.

But I am not the only one who has ever looked around in fear or frustration when the ivory walls closed in around them. And I am not the only one who has made it to the other side without being

---

[3] Oxbridge refers to Cambridge and Oxford.

completely crushed by those walls. Yet, I also recognise that survival often comes from making sacrifices of self and being granted certain privileges. Through all of this, there are those of us who have to tell ourselves that it is okay if all we did today was survive.

This was the story I wanted to share.

At first I planned to write the story with a black male friend from my master's program. I then thought I would write the story alone. As I began to write, however, I felt like something was missing. I was reminded a few weeks into my writing about FLY, the organisation for women of colour at Cambridge I had joined, and the blog in which those women had posted about the very topics I was penning to paper. I knew that without some of those voices added to my own, the telling would be incomplete. Even in this collection of four voices, the telling is incomplete, as there are voices we cannot and should not speak for. I hope that in the sharing of our truths others will do the same for theirs. Collectively we begin to form the narrative that is often pushed to the peripheries of institutions such as Cambridge. However, just as bell hooks wrote, it is in these margins—these peripheries—that we have found our power both individually and together.[4]

It is a deeply peaceful feeling to know that you have spent your time in academia honouring those who go unnoticed despite the work they do each day to survive and make spaces for us. I could never thank Waithera, Lola and Suhaiymah enough for sharing this journey with me. Sometimes I wonder why they accepted the idea to write this book, thrown out to them via a social media chat. I know, however, that they too had stories weighing heavily on their tongues and yearned to speak that truth to power.

In fact, they were already speaking those truths. We just had to find each other.

---

[4] hooks, bell. "Choosing the Margin as a Space of Radical Openness," *Yearning: Race, Gender, and Cultural Politics*. Boston, MA: South End Press, 1990. Print.

To Waithera, Lola and Suhaiymah:

I am honoured to be in your company. I am grateful to share language and stories alongside you all. Our voices have reached further together than they ever could alone. We have so many more stories to tell. May this only be the beginning.

-Odelia S. Younge, Editor
San Francisco, California, USA
April 2016

A FLY Girl's Guide
to University

Dear FLY Girl,

'Why don't you smile more?' they'll ask you.

        'You're one of the chosen ones,' they'll remind you.

So when the professors hand you syllabi with aged inked lists of
     white men

Or the porter stops to ask you who you are,[5]

(Even though you told them yesterday)

(Do you even exist here?)

And you decide to say something

To open your mouth and speak the truths that

Weigh down your tongue

They'll ask you what more do you want?

They'll smile and tell you how grateful you should be

How anyone would want to be in your position

And pierce through your words with eyes that ask again

'What more do you want?'

What do you do?

Do you celebrate the ability to play the game?

You learned the game faster, 'better' than everyone else

You learned to play the part.

How to manipulate the pieces

But as good as you can claim to be,

You did not create these spaces.

And as you learn it, they'll let you win

So they can say

'See, they did it. So can you.'

And your people will say

'They sold out.'

Or, 'They were the chosen one'

They made it out.

---

[5] Porters are the staff members who work in the porter's lodges which are at the entrances of most Cambridge colleges.

But for what?
All you learned was safety.
And how to look at a stranger in the mirror.
You learned how to speak the foreign tongue, sometimes better than
      your mother's tongue.
And you'll wonder if you 'made it'?
Or if they chose you because they thought they could make you.

You could drive yourself mad wondering if anything is ever earned.
You could slit your wrists every night in your nightmares as you
      awake to the 'dream'.
            You could let every instant that they drag up
                to distract you, hurt
             you, make you spend even an ounce of energy on
                feeling any less than human.

You can even say that you found no answers, so the solution must be
      to not ask any questions.
(I have choked on my words, while I swallowed theirs and like acid
      it ate right through my body and rendered my soul
      catatonic)

But there is so much more.
You have to create yourself.
There are worlds beyond the confines of what they tell you is theirs
      and what is yours.

Sharpen your oyster knives, dear sisters.
Slit the noose of white supremacy
Slice through the chords of patriarchy
Slash at every string that threatens to entrap your soul
Your spirit
Your world
Threads that would bind you down and make you choose.

Do not be burdened with their distractions.
You are more than an antithesis.
You can live beyond their grasps.

We are too busy being 'FLY' anyway.

We must learn to heal ourselves
And love again without force or fear.

That is one thing we have always known how to do:
Grow—again—in the midst of the most barren landscapes.

-Odelia Younge

PART ONE:
Revelations

and how strange too, that I speak in a language my grandparents will never understand. that my accent is unrecognizable, that I am white but for my name and colour.

that I use the same words they used so long ago to pacify the natives, that I live in the shadow of a peace that did nothing but burn; the beginning of history in its wake.

-*Jun Pang*

The Breaking and the Making: Becoming Brown
Suhaiymah Manzoor-Khan

It was 8am on A-level results day when my offer to study History at The University of Cambridge was accepted. Almost nineteen, still in my pyjamas, and very much in shock, I could hardly conceive at that time how monumental a change this would be for my life. Not just in all the ways it was supposed to be – not just because it was Cambridge, and not even just because it was university – but more significantly, because Cambridge was the first place I began to think of myself as 'brown'.

Coming from a mixed comprehensive state school in cosmopolitan Leeds, I had rarely experienced being the only brown or Muslim person in a room. Yes, I was aware of being brown; aware of the in-group and the out-group, the difficulties my Pakistani grandparents faced in migrating and the difficulties my parents faced in remaining. I was aware of racist rhetoric, of racism, and the tokenism that followed my successes (often viewed as successes because I was brown and a Muslim). But on the whole, I had a comfortable ride. On the whole, my brownness, and, overlapping with that, my being Muslim, were just parts of who I was. I did Urdu GCSE, I wore a hijab, I used spare classrooms to pray at lunchtimes, and I made jokes about how similar we looked when my white friends came back tanned from holidays. Brownness and Islam were just aspects of my being; just asides to the main spectacle: me.

What changed at Cambridge was that for the first time they weren't just asides, they were the main spectacle. I wasn't just me anymore. First and foremost I was a brown Muslim woman. Arriving there was, as another woman of colour once phrased it, 'like being dropped into a sea of mayonnaise'. Once surrounded and engulfed by whiteness, I not only realised my brownness, I was consumed by it.

I say all this in hindsight. I don't think it hit me immediately. In fact, it took weeks of social anxiety to wonder why people interacted differently with me than they did with others. It took weeks and even months to understand that whilst I was not yet used to having to remember my brownness – to explain and justify it – it was what was first and most apparent to these new strangers.

When people were confronted with me they didn't see the person I knew me to be. What they saw were two things: my hijab and my skin colour. I wouldn't say that every single person treated me as such, but for the many who had clearly never interacted with people who were not white before (or who weren't from private or grammar schools), or those who had gained their only knowledge of Islam and Muslim women from mainstream media, the feeling that I had first to prove my individuality and thus 'humanity' to people, was overwhelming.

It was overwhelming when I was simultaneously battling the fact that student 'normality' was not my normality. Drinking, clubbing, and hoping to 'get with' anyone were not high, or even on, my agenda. Indeed, being a Muslim before Cambridge had often distanced me from 'normality', but the student-stereotype was even further from what I wanted to do or be. How could I prove my humanity when I fell outside the norm of who was 'human' in that space? My abnormality made me Other. I was abnormal every time I asked for the soft drink option instead of 'down[ing] it Fresher!' Every time I went to bed early with time to pray rather than trying to soberly socialise with drunken peers in darkened clubs. Within days I felt ostracised and that I had made no friends.

Of course, this is to some extent, a common feeling for many new university students (had I only known it then). But added to the general experience was the fact I, as a Muslim woman of colour, was specifically excluded from being 'one of the girls'. Though I laugh it off now, it will always perturb me that I was never added to the Facebook chat group set up for 'all' the girls in my college year. Of course there's the petty side of it, but the point I've never managed to articulate to close friends was that for some reason, something prevented me – good or bad – from being included in the bracket, 'the girls'. I was always seen primarily as "Muslim", or 'not white', rather than 'woman' - because 'woman', in that space, was singularly perceived as white. The fact I was a woman who was brown and Muslim destabilised my identity. I existed in a space where I was invisible and confusing because I did not fit the tropes of white femininity. In simply being myself I became an anomaly.

Contrastingly, I felt strangely comfortable around many of the white men in my college. Surprisingly, I even felt at ease, like I was almost 'one of the boys'. In many ways this is a credit to the men I befriended, however, it is certainly not a case of me arguing a misogynistic logic of women being more difficult to befriend. No. Instead I believe that my inability to fit conceptions of white femininity also played into this strange outcome. Under white supremacist patriarchy, white women are the only women deemed 'women', but are also subsequently sexualised for it. My being overlooked as 'woman' seemed to exclude me from the category of 'potential heterosexual partner' in these homogeneously white spaces then. Moreover the legacies of colonialism, orientalism and Islamophobia meant my racialised and hijab-wearing self was excluded from mainstream patriarchal perceptions of beauty, now, sexuality and femininity. In this troubling and convoluted way I found my invisibility as a 'woman' in masculine spaces was what made it possible for me to be disproportionately comfortable around white men; however, that same invisibility felt like uncomfortable hypervisibility in feminine spaces. Therefore, the often intangible forces which so shaped my first-year friendships and socialising were deeply informed by the fact I was not white.

Of course, these theoretical elements of my experience at Cambridge cannot explain everything, and in many ways they are things I have only considered in hindsight. However, what I was aware of at at the time was that the safest I felt in those first few weeks at Cambridge was when I was most able to blend in. This meant that for a long time I hid myself, to protect myself. I internalised the notion that what made me different was also what barred me from 'fitting in'. I internalised the message that I inferred from my surroundings: that I had made it to Cambridge *despite* being a brown Muslim woman.

I became accustomed to being the only person who looked like me in my lectures, at formal meals and in the college bar. I tried to ignore that I was, and I tried to downplay it as much as possible. I handed in every essay on time, stayed very hush-hush about running off to pray throughout the day, always ordered 'vegetarian' rather than the more problematic 'halal'. The safety that came with doing those things – with neutralising what made me stand out – made me believe that others had come to think of me as 'one of them' too. Except they hadn't.

I never became 'one of the girls'. I continued to feel I had to explain myself to porters when entering a college that wasn't mine. I still had to have the extended 'where are you from' conversation: 'Well, I'm from Leeds and my parents are British but my grandparents are from Pakistan, yeah.' I still couldn't really share stories with the same confidence that others could knowing they would be met with nods and agreement. My family, the norms I had never previously thought of as odd, my religion, food, and school all made me feel different. So I hid, as best as possible, many of these things.

In these ways, what I had perceived as safety was actually a loss. A loss because in quieting myself I accommodated prejudice rather than disrupting it and tried to blend in instead of asking people to confront their conceptions of gender, race, Islam or anything else. I allowed people to make me the exception. They made me the one who slipped through the stereotype net. I was likely perceived as the coconut or the not-really-Asian 'Asian'[6]. Therefore, rather than asking for the people

---

[6] Coconut' is a colloquial term sometimes used to refer to people who are, 'brown on the outside but white on the inside'- problematically equating traits, behaviours and ways of speaking to racial logics.

and institution around me to change their workings, the change I made was wholly to myself. I completely internalised what 'fitting in' looked like.

I never considered that success was not the colour of snow and that perhaps I could be my own version. Instead, I swallowed the idea that being a student, doing well in Tripos[7] and rowing down the River Cam were all 'white' things and that in enjoying them I had become less 'authentically' brown. I swallowed the idea that 'cultures' were static, unchangeable realities and that certain traits and behaviours did belong to certain skin-tones. I myself began to believe I was the racial exception. In trying to fit in as a result of the alienation caused by my own identity, I hid my identity. I sold myself short. I ignored my reality rather than claiming it, and the people around me followed suit.

It wasn't until a few months had passed that I began to realise the injustice of all this. Slowly I got tired of pretending and 'fitting in'. I realised that no matter how hard I tried to be Cambridge, Cambridge wouldn't let me be. I could sit in that boat at 6:00am but still feel unseen by the other women. I could be 'taught' to debate at the Cambridge Union but still make my opposition feel confident simply by virtue of not looking like them.[8] I could go to a feminist talk on the harms of pornography but still feel directly othered by an audience member's remark about it being more pertinent to liberate Muslim women who covered their bodies.

It all came to a head. I wasn't fitting in. I couldn't fit in. I couldn't fit in because 'in' was external to me.

So instead I began to ask why so few people at the University of Cambridge looked like me. The wider system of education and social fabric of the country accrued the majority of the blame, but the work Cambridge was doing simply did not feel enough. I became the Access

---

[7] The name for the undergraduate examinations at Cambridge university.
[8] "The Cambridge Union", is the oldest continuously running debating society in the world. It hosts weekly debates between well-known figures on contemporary and contentious topics often for no real consequential reason other than posturing and prestige.

Officer at my college after realising the mass fallacy about 'state school' intake at Cambridge (that the majority of 'state schools' that got pupils into Cambridge were majority-white and middle-class biased grammar schools rather than mixed comprehensives like my own as I'd assumed). But my year in the post was difficult and disillusioning. 'Access' itself felt limited in scope. We emailed many schools but only those responded that already felt Cambridge was achievable. Only those responded whose pupils could easily consider leaving home for University and whose teachers needed no introduction to the 'college system'. This was access, but access to the most accessible. Access to those whose accents would blend in here and whose skin tones would not show up. It was cyclic.

I felt helpless and naive. My mental health deteriorated, my belief in myself dwindled, my self-esteem was a far cry from where it had been in high school, and the fact nobody around me seemed to share in, understand or empathise with my experiences just added to the alienation. I had supposedly 'made it' to the 'height' of academic success, but at what cost to myself? Would I erase myself for a Cambridge education? Would I silence myself and learn to hate my own anger just to defend my own suffering? Yes, things were changing – almost any time I voiced my concerns I was met with 'things are much better than they were a few years ago.' But just because they're better doesn't mean they're good. And just because they're wider doesn't mean they're open.

For me it was no longer fulfilling or right to exist passively at Cambridge. No longer fair that my peers and teachers could be 'blind' to my colour – that I should hide from them stories of racism (and how their own reproductions of it hurt me), and institutional prejudices when my very getting here was against the institutionally-racist-odds. In fact, to be anywhere in a system not built for you is radical and painful. In hindsight I credit myself with this, for even whilst I was not loud about my existence I still existed. And often I was quiet about it because I was afraid and in pain. Not acknowledging that pain was itself an acknowledgement of how deep it was.

But soon enough, the time came when being quiet was not enough. That was how I had slipped under the radar; how I had allowed the institution to pat its own back. While it was not and never will be my sole 'responsibility' to make people change their stereotypes, world-views or institutionally oppressive behaviours and processes, being loud about being othered became a right I had been denying my own soul.

I realised being quiet had allowed people to assume the reason I was one of the few brown or Muslim women here was because I was more like them than I was brown or Muslim. For as long as I did not shout about being brown, as long as I did not make people uncomfortable by excusing myself to go pray salah, as long as I hid the fact I was 'other' and believed myself to be less brown because I was successful, I did a disservice to myself. I let people pretend to forget I was brown and Muslim, let them forget there are systems of inequality, and that injustice is embedded in the fabric of British society. I let them forget I am 'Other'. And I forgot too.

It was in the white spaces of Cambridge then that I consciously came to recognise myself as racialised – that I consciously became 'brown'.

Paki

the first time my brother comes home from school and uses
        the word Paki
i flinch
gasp
almost spill the milk
i tell him
no
that is not a word we use to talk about ourselves

what i do not tell him
what hovers in the space between my words
is that that is a word only other people use about us
a word to crush and hurt us
a word to own us
but not be owned by us

the second time my brother comes home from school
and uses the word Paki
my mother admonishes him
tells him how that word was used to break her bones when
        she was a child
tells him the neighbours would think he had no respect
        for himself if they heard him

what hangs in the air
unspoken
is that that is because Paki deserves no respect
that to say it
might remind them
that our skins are not white
and to our ancestors
this was never home

my grandfather pours over a three inch
pixelated photograph on a phone-screen
cradled in his muscular autumnal hands
hands that taught themselves how cotton was spun
in bradford mills where the lack of light blurred
        young men's sight

hands that held twenty one grandchildren
in a foreign land
to give them hopes and dreams
on these streets paved with gold
and lined with blackened terraced housing

that's not what it looked like when i lived there

the words drop from his mouth
fifty five years heavy with the weight of not forgetting home

the third time my brother comes home from school
and uses the word Paki
i ask him why he is using it pejoratively
why he is synonymising it with filth and sub-par
he says that is the only way he has heard it being used before

the fourth time my brother comes home from school
and uses the word Paki
i smile

i lead him to the kitchen
cut out our tongues
slice them up
and sew them back together in new shapes
relearning the language of our grandmother

i take him to the mirror
show him how to wipe
these ivory-white apologies
from our skins

i stand him in the garden
tell him to look up high
let the sun
work her art
on his beautiful face

we spit out *sorry*
and vomit attempts at assimilation
all over the grass
for assimilation without acceptance
is not that

the rain comes
and washes the dust
from our hands
a colour of pain

and this
is what it is to be a Paki

Pulling the Knife

Waithera Sebatindira

It used to be easy to chart my path from apathetic black girl to angry black woman. Knee-deep in passive aggressive Facebook statuses and think-pieces with which I no longer totally agree, I believed that it was enrolling at Cambridge that made me vocally anti-racist. Then I stumbled upon a sermon I wrote in my final year of sixth form.[9]

In it I called for all of us students to use our privilege to improve the lives of others. To proactively call out racism in our friendship groups, abolish sexist rhetoric in our boarding houses, and refuse to tolerate homophobia. It's hardly a revolutionary message, but I was struck by how much anger lay behind the sermon. I suddenly remembered how desperately I'd hoped the message would be heard by the congregation as I watched the women in my boarding house deliver it.[10] It became clear to me that the reasons why I got so involved in liberation politics at university couldn't be found purely in my time at Cambridge.

This, to me, is an important question because of the nature of the school that I attended from ages 13-17. Private, fee-paying, boarding; I had been sent there by my mother to improve my life chances. And like Cambridge it was predominantly white and middle-class. Racism, both malicious and born of well-meaning ignorance, was far more of a problem there than it ever has been at uni. I experienced more micro-aggressions from people in trusted positions of authority while

---

[9] "Sixth form" denotes the final two years of schooling, after which students can move on to university or Further Education.

[10] Students in boarding schools are often assigned into boarding houses, which can provide accommodation, pastoral care and other services.

at school and felt more isolated from other black students than I do now. I also had no real way to vent my frustrations and no access to the language that would have allowed me to better understand my feelings.

So Cambridge was inevitably the first place where I felt comfortable speaking my truths. It was similar to my school in that I found the same kind of racism there. But I also felt more confident discussing that racism within my college. And the safe space created by FLY allowed me to vent freely, as did access to student press. For the first time since coming to England I had friends who were as eager as I was to organise politically for change.

The language required in order to speak and organise in this way was gifted to me through truly liberating feminist theory that I discovered as a fresher. While at school I read Caitlin Moran's *"How to be a Woman"* (low-key hoping she would literally tell me how to be a woman because I was so bad at it) and Germaine Greer's *"The Female Eunuch"*. I credit these texts with my introduction to feminism, but these were women who were writing for women like them, and not for me. This was something I could sense even as I felt freed by their work. Upon arriving at Cambridge, however, Priscilla pointed me in the direction of Audre Lorde and bell hooks. And life was never the same again.

But strong feelings preceded this access language, and they came long before I could ever hope to articulate them. Finding that sixth form sermon prompted me to properly examine my past. I realised that the necessary, internal conditions for my activism had been laid over the course of my years at private school in England and not in my first few months at Cambridge. Half a decade at that school slowly brought me to terms with a simple truth that was cemented the moment I arrived at Cambridge: that the overwhelming majority of white people occupied a vastly different reality to mine, and that within that reality I would always struggle to be accepted as fully human, and as fully deserving of my achievements.

This conclusion sounds obvious. But I think that reaching it is part of the experiences of many black people when they arrive in white spaces. For me, it is a class issue as well. I get why middle-class black people who come out of spaces like my school and into Cambridge align themselves with racist ideology. I get why black boys undermined my work explaining to white peers why they couldn't say "nigger" by giving permission to all of them to do so. I get why black (usually male) students write articles disparaging anti-racist student organising (usually carried out by women) that goes "too far". This isn't to say that I feel anything other than contempt for them, particularly because many of these people go on to become active participants in institutions that devalue and destroy the lives of people of colour. But I understand them. Because I've come from a similarly suffocating space. I, too, considered pretending racism didn't exist as a means of transcending it among people I knew would never listen to me if I tried to explain how their words and their actions hurt me. And I still continue to unlearn racialized classism – the ease with which I could declare myself "one of the good ones" – everyday.

White institutions – be they universities, secondary schools, or Montessoris – claim to offer us only two choices: break, or be moulded into subservient non-threats to the system. The latter often offers the illusion of power, albeit one that can be taken away at any point and is conditional on you silently swallowing daily racist and sexist humiliations. But there is a third option.

I emerged from my school with an overwhelming desire to tear my university down and build it from scratch using the black feminist principles I quickly learned. I did this not because I was enlightened. I did this because the very nature of these two spaces left me no choice. Minor epiphanies built up over my years at school and made it impossible for me to side with white supremacist logic. That said, it was, in hindsight, a painfully slow process. Unlearning racist ideology is a difficult feat when you are doing it on your own at a private school in the middle of Somerset.

*****

In Year 10, while studying a stained-glass image of White Jesus inside our school chapel, I became suddenly aware of his function in European colonialism and imperialism (I'd been reading about the anthropology of religion at the time and how we tend to make gods in our own image). I recognised the effect that the export by Europeans to Africans of a white God had had on me, a Christian, and the value to which I consequently afforded whiteness. I wondered why it was that I had read Flaubert before Achebe.

Consequently, I decided to decolonise my mind by no longer reading European classics for pleasure and focusing instead on works written by everybody else. Yet, inexplicably, that was the same year that I became heavily involved in the school's Cultural Studies society in which extra-curricular meetings were held where primarily European culture was celebrated. The society itself was largely unproblematic, but while I was blu-tacking poetry about black oppression on the walls of my room to make my white peers uncomfortable, I was also desperately trying to learn how to read Gothic architecture and fall in love with Thomas Tallis. I'd swallowed the belief that those abilities constituted knowledge in which all intelligent people must be well-versed. A fissure had begun to appear in my model minority façade, but it existed as a contradiction alongside my conviction that knowledge of European art was knowledge of some universal and objective truth.

In Year 11, a friend of mine started carrying War and Peace with him around school, partly because he was legitimately ploughing through it and partly to show off. As I watched him walk through the wind tunnel one afternoon with the novel tucked precariously under his arm it suddenly struck me that he would never have used a book by a great black author to demonstrate his precocity. I didn't know whether to feel sad at the thought. Part of me understood why someone like him would choose Tolstoy over Baldwin. At the time, I accepted that certain writers would be celebrated more than others. It was simply the way things were. I didn't think about it again.

By the end of sixth form, white people I had known for five years began calling me by the names of the two other black girls who had joined our class the year before. Friends increasingly demanded that I conform to stereotypes they held of black people. These were the moments that hurt the most. The knowledge that I could spend years making myself known to those around me, only to discover that the racist ideas I thought I was dispelling were merely lying dormant. And yet even this was not enough to drill in the truth of our fundamentally different realities. Because, saddened as I was by my friends' behaviour, little of it was truly surprising. I had to be hit not so much where it truly hurt but by those who I had genuinely believed knew better.

It was our final Cultural Studies outing of the year. We'd spent the afternoon exploring the ruins of a local abbey before heading for dinner. Before we ate, we sat around a piano and our teacher, the head of the society, taught us "Gaudeamus Igitur"[11] and it was all very emotional given that we would soon be leaving school and heading to university. All was going well until he suggested we sing "Rule, Britannia".[12] I froze. "Rule, Britannia"? That refrain celebrating the fact that Britons would never be slaves, composed around a point in history when their country was transporting an average of 42,000 Africans across the Atlantic?[13] I had absolutely no desire to sing it.

I was left with three options. I could let everyone know that they were free to sing the song (I lacked both the confidence and the language to explain the issues I had with imperial nostalgia) but state that I would not be joining in and give my reasons. This would likely have led to awkwardness and the room feeling that I had ruined a perfectly good evening with my talk of slavery.

Option number two involved hiding in the bathroom until they were

---

[11] A popular Latin song usually sung at academic graduation ceremonies.

[12] A British patriotic song. Its lyrics originate from a poem and were set to music in 1740.

[13] Mohamud, A. and Whitburn, R. (2018). Britain's involvement with New World slavery and the transatlantic slave trade. [online] British Library. Available at: https://www.bl.uk/restoration-18th-century-literature/articles/britains-involvement-with-new-world-slavery-and-the-transatlantic-slave-trade# [Accessed 12 Dec. 2018].

done singing the song. But I knew I'd then be in there for an awkwardly long amount of time...

So it was the third option. Sing the song and feel like a coward. Which I did, although I also found some humour in the ridiculousness of my situation.

Beyond shame, though (beyond humour, beyond me) I realised - properly internalised - for the first time that these people who were my friends and mentor occupied an entirely different reality to mine. This was odd because our stories were in many ways so intimately tied to each other. Slaves packed tightly into ships, choked by the smell of death, listening to creaking boards and the footsteps of their captors on the deck above. Kenyan children returning home from boarding school to find their homes turned into concentration villages, their parents tortured in concentration camps. Everything in between. These sets of facts happened to all of us. They are our shared history. But we had such fundamentally different memories of these objective facts that it didn't occur to a single one of them that I would have no desire to sing a song glorifying that past.

More insidiously, I understood exactly why they would want to sing that song. I had a very good understanding of how they viewed that past and it came to me immediately. But the same could not be said of them. I knew instinctively in that moment that even if I tried to explain why I didn't want to sing that song most, if not all, of them wouldn't understand. It would simply be political correctness gone mad.

Later that evening (after I'd decided to put the song at the back of my mind), I was reminded of what was then one of my proudest moments, which had occurred around twenty-four hours prior. I had given a Cultural Studies talk on emotions. It was packed with fairly pointless factoids, one of which was that men allegedly have an easier time communicating side-by-side while women supposedly prefer talking face-to-face. The talk was well-received by everyone in attendance. I gave it shortly after I'd received an offer to study at Cambridge, and our teacher went as far as to tell me that my presentation was better than what he'd usually heard discussed by his peers during his own time as an undergraduate there.

After we'd sung about slavers never being slaves we sat down for dinner and one of the talk attendees turned to our teacher and said: "Did you know that men have an easier time talking side-by-side while women prefer to talk face-to-face?"

He said it as if he was providing new information to the group, most of whom had attended my talk the evening prior. Our teacher then stated that he had heard that before but didn't know where. I then watched them debate over where they could possibly have come across this fact. Both were convinced it was from a documentary they'd recently watched, but our teacher didn't own a TV so how could that be?

It took me the longest time to realise they weren't joking. For one wild second I wondered if I'd imagined giving the talk. Someone else in the group had to point out that I was the one who had informed them of that fact just over twenty-four hours earlier.

In those moments I felt invisible. I saw a world where somehow my hours of research and preparation could exist while I myself was not in the picture. I was erased.

What hurt most, though, was the apology. After the two of them had realised their mistake one said that my presentation was so good that they'd unconsciously attributed it to someone else. This back-handed compliment could have merely been a personal insult were it not for its context. One in which nothing similar had happened to white students who had given similar talks.

It was an apology also contextualised by the years prior to it during which people had frequently separated my body from my person with ease. That is, I was surrounded by people who could know me as Audrey (the name by which I used to go) with all of my unique characteristics, but also forgot me entirely and speak to me generically as if I was any black girl. From being told by a teacher I thought knew me well that I should pursue journalism to write about racism, despite never having expressed an interest in the subject at the time, to having friends regularly forget everything they knew about me in order to crush me into racist caricatures.

I could pull out so many receipts of moments when those around me would reduce me to stereotypes when only minutes before they'd been addressing me as a person with a three-dimensional personality. The issue wasn't that they were conscious of my race; I want my heritage to be recognised and appreciated where relevant. The problem was that no one ever tried to see how my being black shaped me as an individual. Instead, even those who knew me well imposed their own ready-made conceptions of blackness, completely different from who I actually was. I felt like they alternated between two extremes when they saw me: either through a colour-blind lens, thereby making me one of them, or through a racialized one, making me other.
I remember smaller moments, too. Ones of which I'm slightly less certain but that remain firm in my memory and make me pause. Of being held behind in a maths lesson after I'd scored the highest mark in a test and gently interrogated as to how I'd managed it before the teacher simply conceded: "You're just clever, aren't you?" Of the same rhetorical question later being posed by my tutor as she looked over my grades that term.

I remember complaining to a white male classmate (now a fellow Cambridge alumnus) about how I'd been accused by a friend of stealing an imaginative idea for which I'd been praised by our English teacher. He joked that, by contrast, whenever he came up with something original people asked him if he'd written a book on it. It was a hyperbole, but it was rooted in truth. I stared at his laughing face and genuinely wondered why our ideas received such different reactions.

Being attention-hungry, I always played the fool in class. This I know played its part in my being underestimated. But my academic ability was always apparent in my grades and in the fact that I was often right when I raised my hand in class. The level of surprise engendered by my Cambridge offer thus confused me and made me resentful. And while these moments were relatively rare, they remain fleeting occurrences that I find myself, years later, still contemplating.

So when I was told that my talk was so good it had been attributed to someone else, what I heard was this: we are so unused to valuing knowledge from people like you that we unconsciously attributed it to an imaginary (probably white, male) person who would be more likely to produce valuable knowledge. Even though they accepted that a mind like mine could produce an enjoyable talk, they had too rarely been exposed to the idea that a body like mine could produce it, as well. And when the body was removed in order to make the knowledge's context more intelligible, so, too, was I.

Combined with the fact that it did not occur to them that I would not want to sing a slaving society's victory call, I could finally disinvest from them. Every minor (and major) racist incident that I dismissed as individual coagulated into a culture I shouldn't have had to endure. Every suspicion I had secretly held that these people might never truly see me as an individual was validated. I was still afraid of speaking out but I did suddenly become aware of a knife lodged in my gut. I noticed for the first time that over the course of the last five years an imaginary hand had been slowly, slowly twisting it. The blade's trajectory mapped my growing knowledge that my peers, who I loved, occupied a different world and that, within it, it was apparently incredibly difficult for a black woman to be understood as a complex, valuable, intelligent human being – to be deemed worthy of learning from.

I went to Cambridge and it was confirmed to me almost immediately that the knife was expected to be a normal part of my life. I could accumulate degrees, garner multiple successes, and my black woman's work and my black woman's body would still too rarely receive the respect they deserved. So, within weeks of arriving at Cambridge, I pulled at the knife with everything I had. And it all came spilling out.

Shifting Perspectives and Challenging Representations
Odelia Younge

I spent the summer before my senior year of high school in the shadows of Cambridge's majestic buildings. It was a momentous time in my life, as it was the first time I had been out of the country since my family first arrived to the U.S. in 1993. That summer was also the first time I was surrounded by children who came from wealth and privilege. No one knew I did not, as the program did not advertise that I was on financial aid, and I did not supply the information. For that summer I just wanted to enjoy the life we were living without having others creating lines of 'other' around me. Cambridge was a place of exploration and finding ways to exist in spaces not meant for me. It is a lesson I have come to know time and time again. I vowed to go back to the lush green expanses, majestic towers and looming old buildings of Cambridge one day. It wouldn't be until a decade later that I would make good on that promise. Instead, I found myself in the 'other' Cambridge: Cambridge, Massachusetts at Harvard for my undergraduate studies.

The world of Harvard and the majority of its students was foreign to me. I was a black, immigrant woman who grew up in a liberal, low-income family of seven that was (for the majority of my childhood) the only non-white family in the surrounding school district of rural, conservative Indiana. After a series of events, we had found ourselves in this small, isolated part of the earth. I don't know what my parents knew of this world, but I do know what they hoped for their children. It was that hope that encapsulated us throughout our childhood, and it was that hope that led my mother to leave a Harvard application on my desk my senior year of high school. Immigrant parents dream of worlds for their children that they never knew. Black immigrant parents seek a world that may let their children live a little longer. Sometimes the Diaspora is created from desperation as well as hope and devastation.

I was raised to have faith and to be fearless. Faith in the journey God had set out for me and fearless of others' attitudes toward me because of that faith. This was not without caution. I was not sheltered from the evils of this world or the dangers in carrying this dark skin, especially while surrounded by Confederate flags and racist rhetoric. But I was raised by a woman who is multiethnic, with straight hair and light skin, but who always deliberately raised black children. One might say, of course your mother raised a black child, look at you. My dark skin and features cannot hide. But many people with black children do not raise black children. When I say 'raise a black child,' I mean bringing them up to know love and to be loved. That though there is danger in this dark skin, that is not from us. This dark skin is the source of our deepest powers. Harriet Tubman was my first hero. I have always kept her words close to me: "God's time is always near. He meant I should be free." [14]

So my four years at Harvard became a time of continuously shifting perspectives and framing. It was the first time I was consistently around people who looked like me who were not related to me. The first time I had incredible access to journals, books, and professors that challenged me to go deeper. But I enjoyed those things later. I spent the first half of my freshman year feeling out of place and stressed with the systems at play. I had teaching fellows who would not support me in my learning, and I was constantly reminded of the privileges that others around me had been afforded that left them heirs to the elite thrones of universities like Harvard. It wasn't until I started engaging Harvard on my own terms, recognising that I had learned to curate my survival in rural Indiana and could do so here too,

[14] Harriet Tubman to Ednah Dow Cheney, New York City, circa 1859.

that I found the spaces that I thrived. I stopped thinking about fighting battles and shifted my perspective to focus on building, on cultivating, on *creating myself to freedom*. 'Creating myself to freedom' is about unlearning what others have said is true of myself and the world and to unleash my own vision of self into the world.

So when Cambridge and I met again for my graduate studies almost a decade after our first encounter, I had learned how to exist in places not meant for me without giving up critical elements of my being. I had come back with a suitcase filled with questions that I wanted the distance from the U.S. and the time to explore. At the end of the first meeting of my 15-person thematic route in the Education Faculty on Politics, Development, and Democratic Education (PDDE), the head of the route—who was also my supervisor—told us that we would have to dig deep within ourselves to find a place that allows us to keep our idealism in the face of an onslaught of heavy criticism. I smiled as I wrote down her words in the cover of my notebook that Zadie Smith would later grace with her signature after a talk that made me come back to what my supervisor first said.

I understood my supervisor's words because it was what any passionate educator does. We work tirelessly for our students – our children – in the face of a relentless onslaught from conflicted school administrators, and politics and bureaucracy that have tried everything to ensure that a joy of learning is stomped out of school systems. It would make even the biggest and warmest of hearts fall prey to the dark depressions of October onward during the school year. It takes support from colleagues, becoming part of a community, and the faces of your students to keep that idealism that things could be different.

What I loved most about the introduction to my course was that it honoured the perspectives that challenged and asked for us to deeply engage with them. During one session of my research methods class they showed us a map of the London tube. It was a very dense map of all the stations that the tube has and looked like it covered a large part of London. Then, the instructor showed us another map. This map was a geographical map of the London tube which showed how close particular neighborhoods were to each other that the Tube map made look far from one another. It also showed all the areas that went without underground rail service. The third map the instructor showed us was a map of the wheelchair accessible service of the tube. There were very few stations that were wheelchair accessible, and it was obvious how hard it would be to get from one point to another. In fact, when the tube was out of service and people were complaining about the stops that were not operating, one handicapped individual said that it was how the tube looked to them every day.

That's perspective.

What the instructor challenged us to examine was the idea of representations of truth. She said that the more we knew – such as in the case of seeing different perspectives of the London tube map – the more we would question the notion that sources are reliable. I understand that there are different value systems and different view -points in life. However, such systems should never question or oppress the humanity of any group of people; should always work toward the emancipation of oppressed and marginalised selves. Should always, at its core, seek to eradicate anti-blackness. The more maps we look at, the more we should be willing to look at things differently.

However, as my time went along in PDDE, I found that the ability to truly examine the world around us often got lost. The 'acceptable' liberal views on the topics we discussed were pushed forward, approved, and the class moved on. Nuances were shied away from that are aligned with more radical, liberating politics. Some might claim that they put forth such radical worldviews, but they were ones that were built from the imaginations of white men. You can't build a new world from tools that only know the blueprints of oppression.

On some days it felt like a series of watching people go around and give each other academic high-fives. We did not speak as much on race and gender as we should have, seldom engaging with how they impact who we educate and how we educate, and to what ends, and how gender and race are used as the vessels to create failing systems. Whenever we did talk about race and gender the conversation was shallow at best, never diving into the murky yet clear waters of history. Was it that some felt guilty about their own positions or thought they had already done the hard work of decolonising their positions? I can't say absolutely, but I will assume, with enough evidence, that this played a significant role. While some were willing to engage in deeper conversations outside of class, it still left the classroom devoid of necessary uncomfortable conversations.

The majority of students I encountered at Cambridge prided themselves in presenting as open-minded, even when so many were not. Conversations became about who had read the densest books, instead of who had actively tried to push back on systems. They became about who could sound the most 'learned,' instead of who had taken the time sit with the realities of the narratives of those they spoke about and those they believed they had a right to speak for.

One coursemate gave a talk on his time teaching abroad in Africa and how he felt torn about being there and the history of colonialism he was engaging with and the harm his presence had possibly done. I looked around at everyone nodding along to his 'harrowing' tale of whiteness abroad. I raised my hand during the question portion and asked him why he was incapable of seeing the members of the community he worked in as people with agency. Yes, they have been impacted by years of Western presence but that did not mean they could not have found their own ways of 'using' or dismissing the people who had used them for so long. Perhaps they were getting what they wanted and it was not a one-way street of power. I pointed out to him that by assuming what his role in the process was, he had, in fact, centred himself in the narrative once more. He had told a story that was about the magnitude of whiteness, asserting that it was so powerful it shook the very ground people walked on for the few months he had been there.

This was a common story I heard across the university from students who had spent time abroad. It was only slightly better than those who were well travelled yet had never taken the time to talk to the people in the countries they visited, preferring to hole themselves up behind walls that expats dream of. Nevertheless, they were the central source on the happenings of the world because they had read about it. What was found in books—though the books were written by people they generally felt safe reading—was enough to make them experts on the lives of others. Making people listen when I had something to share about my lived experiences instead of having them genuinely invite me to speak on these matters, left me with the bitter taste that one finds in their mouth when confronted by people who declare themselves 'ally', yet turn around and silence and disregard the very people they proclaim to support.

What are 'elite' universities, but oftentimes a microcosm of the power dynamics of the larger world around them? Who gets in, what makes its way onto the curriculum, what is celebrated as rigorous debate and discourse. Many professors rarely pushed back on any of this as well, which was especially reflected in our curriculum. The classic Cambridge curriculum is a who's who of white males who "think" about things and people believe them. White males who write about themselves and white males who write about the 'other'. Whether it was research methods or a discussion of politics, I found myself wondering about how people who spoke from the point of view of people like me saw the world through these topics. I had to return to the lessons learned during undergraduate and sought those perspectives myself.

In Michaelmas term,[15] I wrote my first paper on the potential positive impacts of Afrocentric education on black children in the U.S. One of my two markers used more than half of her written remarks to discuss that although markers were advised not to influence the scholarship students chose to engage with, whilst simultaneously penning a long

---

[15] Michaelmas is the first term at Cambridge, lasting from end of September/beginning of October until early December.

list of scholars she would have liked me to have engaged in my paper. Many on her list were not black, or even people of colour, and were mainly men. I had written a paper on *Afrocentric education* and its aims of decentering whiteness and Eurocentrism, yet it was perceived that there was a problem with *my* scholarship when over 80% of my bibliography consisted of black scholars.

These scholars were probably people the marker was not familiar with, and the Cambridge canon — cradled by its mother, the Western canon — could not conceive of scholars who were not readily used by them. Even when they discussed "cutting edge" new scholars speaking on theories that shifted from the mainstream, many of them were still white. These scholars became the voices that worked to erase scholars of colour writing from the perspective of one who has lived experiences. Positioning white scholars as the authoritative voice draws the academy away from scholars of colour who are actively choosing to break the cycles of representation that deem works produced by them as 'less-than'.

We are not allowed to be experts. Given the chance, we are excluded for fear of what we may say that could make others uncomfortable or the undeniable and hard truths we may state. Our mere presence is enough to elicit this fear. When Zoey, one of my best friends from Harvard, came to visit in the spring, we went to a talk by Zadie Smith that the English Faculty was hosting. We were both excited since we were familiar with Smith's works. By Cambridge standards, the room was filled with many students of colour, which I thought was a great sign. Then I saw who was hosting the event, the one who would get to sit next to Zadie and ask her questions: a white student. This was incredibly frustrating because in a place such as Cambridge — with a less than 3% black population, where being represented comes down to a token BME student on a university brochure — when someone who gives fills you with pride and joy because of what she has accomplished comes along in an accessible format, the university provides a gatekeeper to keep this interaction at bay. There are students of colour in the English Faculty. There are students of colour in the humanities in general. But nothing can belong to us, not even our own.

As if it was not enough that this student was given this privileged position over others, she did not come prepared. She was only vaguely familiar with the complexities of Smith's characters and themes. Her questions revealed an absence of knowledge of the connection between Smith's journey throughout her time at Cambridge, steeped in its ancient curricula, and her life as a black woman in the UK, to her ability to reimagine the possible in her writing. The moderator's questions were shallow and binary. I knew this was not just in my head because Zoey and I later discussed at length Smith's subtle to not-so-subtle side-eyeing of her interviewer and curt answers to the silliest questions that had the most obvious answers.

However, Zadie Smith was everything we wanted her to be — she was brilliant! She talked about how she felt she had to take on masculine characteristics to succeed academically and achieve first class honours.[16] She talked about her children's dual nationalities and identities, and the process of bringing to life the characters in her writing. When the interviewer continued making statements pushing how Smith must have this imaginative and innovative approach to writing new things, Zadie responded that sometimes she wrote things that were good, and sometimes she wrote things that were not. In fact, she doesn't truly love her first novel, yet it is the one people ask her about the most. Entering Smith's story from the first written chapter, people forget everything she was and everything else she has become.

Zadie Smith didn't need to be a superhero black woman author. It was such a relief to hear. Even in the midst of the type of white feminist allyship the interviewer wished to extend, Zadie Smith remained in her truth. I can only guess that she had learned to challenge representations that others had of her a long time ago, and especially at Cambridge. 'Sometimes you get a flash of what you look look like to other people.'[17]

---

[16] This is the highest mark an undergraduate can earn in their studies at Cambridge.
[17] From Zadie Smith, *On Beauty*, 2005

We have to challenge the representations that exist. For so long, on a macro and micro level, there have only been the voices of those in power. We have to find the sweet spot between knowing that what is represented can be skewed by those in power, but also acknowledging that as humans, we need to represent ideas and issues for people to engage them. It is a problem and a paradox. But it's also what inspired me to shift my research focus to finding out more about how marginalised youth challenge these representations. And it's also what inspired me to build out a research methodology that would allow their representations to challenge and supersede any analysis that I might do.

I have always been taught by my mother and the educators that I have come to treasure that questions of narratives and representations determine the role of the historian and the researcher. Maybe my role as a black woman historian and researcher is to connect with and bring to the forefront these stories and studies of my people. Though I don't know if I am doing any of it right, I know that I take my role as one who represents and whose representations are sometimes taken seriously as if my life depends on it—and in many ways it does. I want to be a voice amongst the marginalised, but I don't want to be that voice either. It is a careful road to walk on that takes continuous discourse and a life and work that meet that challenge, no matter what institutions beg it not to or do not provide the spaces for the work.

Why I'm Done Defending my Personhood: 3rd January 2015
Lola Olufemi

The article below is the first full length piece I wrote about my experience at Cambridge and was published on the Fly Blog in 2015.

Since coming to Cambridge I've had numerous conversations, usually with white boys, who "just don't get it." Boys who have never thought critically about race or gender and are unable to see themselves as complicit in the oppression of marginalised groups. They struggle to understand the immense power that is afforded to them by virtue of what they look like. I have always been open to having conversations about what race and gender mean in real terms and how they affect the lives of individuals on a daily basis, I enjoy bursting the bubble of idealism that these boys exist in. I like asking hard questions because making people feel uncomfortable is a radical way to get them to recognise the existence of oppressive systems. In no place is this bubble of idealism more apparent than in Cambridge. When you've had too much to drink after formal and you have to explain the history of racial oppression in America to a white boy who tells you "Darren Wilson[18] is a person too" or when you drop the shocker that "reverse racism" and "sexism against men" are fallacies, it is exhausting. Any criticism of white supremacy is often taken personally: "But, I'm a nice guy so I don't know what you're talking about." "You can't generalise." One of my favourites is the attempt to completely erase erase identity: "Why do you always talk about white and black, there is

---

[18] On the 9th August, 2014, Michael Brown, an 18 year old black boy was shot and killed by Darren Wilson, a white police officer in the city of Ferguson Missouri. The event sparked unrest in Ferguson with protesters drawing attention to police brutality, racist police practices and the militarisation of policing in the suburb.

only one race – the human race."

When your friends start singing "Do they Know It's Christmas?"[19], you're faced with the choice of ruining the mood by pointing out that the lyrics of that song reinforce an image of Africa as disease-ridden, poverty-stricken and in need of white saviours or just singing along. As we become politicised, it is important to figure out what our personal role in liberation is. Is it to educate white boys about structural racism? To some extent, yes – consciousness raising is the job of everyone who is politically engaged. But, I am slowly starting to realise something and want to share it with the women of colour in my life: Do not ever feel guilty for letting a racist joke slide because you couldn't think of something to neutralise the situation in time.

It is not your job to defend your personhood when it is under attack. Do not waste your breath attempting to convince individuals that you too deserve respect. It is like repeatedly hitting your head against a brick wall. Yes, you might eventually begin to chip away at it, but you do more damage to yourself in the process. Your dignity as a human being is not up for debate. Use the energy you conserve to organise. Protest. Speak only to people who are willing to listen to you without becoming defensive or overly argumentative; people who are genuinely interested in understanding the world from your perspective. You are allowed to be tired. You are a human being who lives in a system in which you experience violence at every turn, protecting yourself fiercely is of the utmost important.

My own experiences as a black working class girl have informed my understanding of how race, sex and class operate within a wider systematic framework. Since coming to Cambridge, because of whiteness and the overwhelming number of male dominated spaces, everything is more political and it is truly a joy. There are spaces at this university where oppressed people come together to provide support and solidarity for one another, examine our conditions and develop

---

19 "Do They Know It's Christmas?" is a song written in 1984 by Bob Geldof and Midge Ure in reaction to television reports of the 1983–1985 famine in Ethiopia.

our understanding of truly liberatory politics. These spaces help mitigate the burden of existing in a space that sometimes might not feel completely our own.

It should go without saying that the white boys I refer to in this article are 'well meaning', middle class, cis, heterosexual males who truly believe that they got into Cambridge purely on academic merit and nothing else. It is a mix of naivety, entitlement and ignorance. I've often wondered if they can be blamed for their own misconceptions. If they have never been exposed to the realities of structural oppression, if they have been born into comfortable lifestyles that refuse to look outward – why would they be concerned with the lived experience of a black woman? Or a working class trans woman? But they are big boys now. They're at university. They have a responsibility to educate themselves. It is not our job as women of colour to politely coax them into agreeing with us.

I'm slowly realising that educating others should not be our primary concern. Existing and attempting to have full and creative lives should. We should be generating material that helps to counteract the decades in which our voices have been silenced. You shouldn't be tiring yourself out wondering if you took your argument too far in the debate last night, or if all the boys will think of you as "the angry black girl." Embrace the label and carry on.

PART TWO:

How We Speak and Who We Speak For

"Skin like porcelain"; I wonder why
The metaphors you pen make me so
Breakable.

--Jun Pang

Academia and Unbearable Whiteness

Lola Olufemi

Why is my curriculum white?" is a question I did not ask myself until the end of my first year at university. I spent most of the year posturing, ascribing more importance to the white men that I learnt about than was necessary and being taught that literary theory and criticism had to be apolitical to be valuable. This question becomes more pertinent each year. As a person of colour studying a subject dominated by white faces, the Eurocentric curriculum acts as another reminder that what we value as literary critics, as historians, as scientists, the kinds of knowledge we deem worthy of study, have been shaped by the structurally oppressive nature of society. Much of 'high culture' and our understanding of cultural capital depends upon the praise of knowledge produced in a white, Western framework and the derision of works from the Global South.

When I, as an English student, cannot formally study a single person who looks like me for the first two years of my degree, what I am being subjected to is a violent form of erasure. People of colour, women, queer and trans people and those of us who are all of these things at the same time are being written out of history, our contributions ignored. This becomes so normalised that our invisibility is not even discussed, not addressed and laughed off in lectures. That you are considered a silent nuisance if you insist on reaching for queer or postcolonial texts, or refuse to treat them as universal in your weekly essay, speaks volumes.

Being made to study the work of white men without a critical framework that allows us to question these texts results in the maintenance of the power and cultural dominance that underpinned the creation of English Literature as a discipline. This dominance is so insidious that our idea of 'high culture' is often defined by how many white male writers we can rattle off at parties. "Well, have you read Foucault?" "Do you like Auden? Proust?" and so on.

This isn't to say that white men have not contributed anything to our understandings of the world, but simply that it is ludicrous to treat their works as if they are the only seminal texts. If the clothes we wear, the desks we sit at, the institutions to which we belong, if all of these things have been made possible through the exploitation of former colonies and the global south, then we have a moral duty — at the very least — to treat the ideas of those people with dignity. We should consider them robustly and in place of standard European texts. This is about more than tokenism. It is not enough to throw *Things Fall Apart* onto the reading list. We have to first address the ideological reasons behind this institution's insistence on relying on a singular form of knowledge production and then radically transform our curricula and democratise the university to address it.

We do this not only by including a range of voices and experiences in our study, but also by expanding our idea of what is worthy of study. We must do away with the snobbery attached to "lower forms" of literature and art; what is needed is serious critical engagement with them. How do the real life experiences of grassroots scholars impact academia? Is there space for political and feminist readings of You-Tube videos, blogs? Space for the consideration of all forms of knowledge that exist outside of the white male paradigm? An understanding that feeling and ways of being are just as important as a means of acquiring knowledge as detached rationality?

If we continue to study one kind of knowledge, our ideas not only become stagnant but we advance frameworks of thinking that refuse to admit the very real differences between us. It is useless to pretend that Dickens "spoke the language of humanity" or that white male authors can articulate other experiences unaffected by their positionality. The effect of the white curriculum is such that we have imbued white male writers with the power and authority to speak for everyone; marginalised students often find themselves grasping at texts that were not written for them in an attempt to find a shared humanity that is based on their exclusion. We must rid ourselves of the idea that there is an inherent value in studying texts that are violently misogynistic or racist without acknowledging that they do great harm to their readers. If we are asked to study aestheticised depictions of violence against women, from domestic violence to rape, but refuse to look at such texts through a critical framework and instead insist on seeing them as "art for art's sake", we contribute to a society that valorises masculinist ways of thinking and enables rape culture. We treat sexual violence as if it were a thing of the past, ignoring the fact that women in the classroom will have experienced it.

What we study and how we study it is important because it shapes the lens through which we see the world. If we only view the world through the eyes of the powerful, if our curricula continue to rely on the ideas of white men, that lens is clouded and becomes harmful to other people. There are scholars at grassroots levels, working in community centres, hospitals and youth groups doing the same kind of intellectual work as those trapped in the ivory tower; it is just that we are better able to recognise an article or a peer-reviewed journal than we are the merits of work on the ground. We must think about ways we can transform and decentre the university as the only site of legitimate knowledge production. This is not just about stepping aside to 'let new voices in': they must be afforded the entire stage.[20]

---

[20] This article marked the beginning of questions around decolonising curricula in the English Faculty which are explored in more detail in the last chapter.

Language
Waithera Sebatindira

My mum bought me lifetime membership to the Union during freshers' week in the hope that I would make all the right connections there. With hindsight, I wish I'd known to ask her not to because I almost never attended its talks or debates. Among the exceptions to this rule was an interview-type session with a famous CNN journalist whose face had featured prominently on the living room TV screen at home during my childhood and adolescent years.

Her talk was interesting. She deliberated over issues surrounding free speech, journalist herd mentality. I felt inspired in the way one usually feels inspired when in the presence of someone with great achievements. That was until she started discussing the genocides she'd covered in Bosnia and Rwanda. I was put off - mainly by her language.

When speaking about Bosnia, her language was relatively objective. She talked about meeting women and children there and was frank about how she'd intended to help hold their government accountable. She briefly mentioned the massacres, although there was little mention on her part of the people actually carrying out the killing. She spoke matter-of-factly about how Bosnia represented the first time that journalists were threatened and attacked for being journalists.

When she moved on to Rwanda, her language became far more emotive. With no mention of the victims of the genocide, no allusion to the political conditions that brought it about, she ripped into the Rwandans. In quick succession out came these words from her mouth: "primitive", "pre-industrial", and "savage". She described her worrries about being dragged out of her van at checkpoints and "clubbed over the head". She spoke as if the Rwandan genocide was somehow more horrific because she didn't view the violence carried out as being calculated and organised in the way that European genocides are.

I wasn't there. Her fear must have been great. It's obvious that the reason she spoke more strongly about Rwanda is because she genuinely feared more for her life there than in Bosnia. This isn't really about her.

I sighed when she spoke those words because they're so common coming from the mouths of non-Africans: "primitive", "pre-industrial", "savage". Words stored specifically in that part of the brain marked "knowledge about Africa". Like most intelligent speakers, she often paused to find the right words with which to describe her thoughts and experiences. There was no pause when she spoke of Rwanda.

She's not the only one who has bought into this imagery. Earlier that week, the Daily Mail featured a racist caricature of Africans that could have come from a British newspaper published in the 1950s.[21] Its depiction perfectly matched the liberal journalist's words. There were Africans selling disembodied heads, bones through their noses, wearing animal skins, in a jungle somewhere. A cartoon with no real object. Just an excuse to portray Africans in the usual way. As primitive, pre-industrial, and savage.

The fact that a liberal journalist and a right-wing newspaper can use exactly the same imagery to describe one group of people (and only that group of people) goes to show just how inured we've become to this rhetoric surrounding Africa. In the eyes of most these words aren't political – they're axiomatic. Woven into the Western culture they all share so that when they turn their gaze to the Dark Continent they see what they always expected to see: that we Africans are primitive, pre-industrial, and savage.

---

[21] https://www.huffingtonpost.co.uk/2015/11/03/daily-mail-mac-cartoon-tom-jones-race-black_n_8460604.html

These are words I hear to describe my continent even when there is no conceivable reason why they would be necessary or appropriate. In a *Daily Mail* article about a plane crash in South Sudan, the unrelated fact that the country is currently facing a war had to be tacked on at the end.[22] When Barack Obama visited Nairobi for the 2015 Global Entrepreneurship Summit, CNN felt compelled to refer to Kenya as a 'terror hotbed'.[23] A claim that was just as untrue as it was unnecessary. I could spend forever pulling out receipts, but look at any article on any country in sub-Saharan Africa by any non-African author and it's extremely likely that somewhere, somehow there'll be a reference to extreme poverty or war. Just in case the reader was at risk of forgetting even for a second that Africans are primitive, pre-industrial, and savage.

I repeat these words because I want you, the reader, to really look at them. Feel their weight and fully understand just how offensive they are. Words are never meaningless when they are backed by centuries of oppression and continued displacement, exploitation, and violence. That these are the same words that are repeated time and time again, the same evocations of imagery over and over, is clearly further evidence that there is something to their particular meaning. Something very specific is being said. One idea perpetuated. These words aren't spoken in a vacuum. They carry luggage. Let's unpack some of it:

Primitive

I've found that the strongest connotation behind this word is one of a lack of intelligence. There's this belief that Africans are dim-witted and that this is in itself why the continent appears so poor. This kind of reasoning lies behind neo-eugenic arguments against allowing the migration of Africans into Western countries. It fuels counter-

---

[22] https://www.dailymail.co.uk/news/article-3303160/Russian-plane-crashes-taking-airport-South-Sudan-killing-10-people.html
[23] https://www.iol.co.za/news/africa/cnn-calls-kenya-a-hotbed-of-terror-1890492

productive development programmes that treat us as being incapable of agency or the same level of rational thought as our European counterparts.

It allows the rest of the world to devalue our work, because primitive people cannot produce anything worthy of critical intellectual engagement. Instead our art and literature is widely viewed from an anthropological rather than appreciative perspective. To take just one example, there are ancient bronze sculptures from Benin that objectively aesthetically rival anything produced by Degas and the like. But the former will never receive the recognition they deserve (at least not in our lifetimes). This is because part of the appeal of art is the genius of the mind that produced it, but genius cannot exist in a primitive mind. While European artists are credited for the discipline, hard work, and knowledge behind their art, the inspiration for African art is always seen as being somehow raw. Impressive, but unpolished. Wholly accidental. And its value is diminished accordingly.

This word "primitive" is often applied more generally to African cultures. In her essay "Can the White Girl Twerk", Ayesha Siddiqi points out that, in the context of cultural appropriation, white culture is often deemed to be rooted in intent, while non-white culture is seen as being rooted in instinct.[24] That is, white people do what they do because they have chosen to do it, whereas non-white people simply don't know any better. I feel like this applies strongly outside of the context of cultural appropriation as well, and provides an excellent analysis for understanding how non-Africans view us. Again, we Africans are robbed of our agency through the constant use of this word and in a way we're robbed of our culture, too. In the sense that it is deemed ours because we happened upon it by instinct, rather than because we carefully formed it. This partially (if not wholly) explains how non-Africans feel able to take and distort African cultures, defining them for themselves and taking no account of how Africans

---

[24] Siddiqi, Ayesha, *"Can the White Girl Twerk"* https://thenewinquiry.com/can-the-white-girl-twerk/

feel about this misappropriation. Put into the context of capitalist power dynamics, Westerners are able to profit off of our stolen ideas, use our erasure to shore up proof of their own capacity for innovation, and draw money and prestige away from those who are truly entitled to it. Having been forcibly subjected to the global market this is one of the many ways that we are excluded from its spoils. We can ask philosophical questions about whether art or culture should be to capitalist thinking but the cold, hard truth is that is. White people who misappropriate our culture for their own profit and have no intention of directing attention and wealth to Africans are no better than their ancestral colonialists.

The fact that our continent birthed the longest-running empire in human history is completely ignored in favour of ingrained modern myths about our primitive incompetence. Our contributions to history convincingly white-washed or trivialised, because no primitive mind could have given humankind anything of value. In this way our histories are stolen from us as well as from the rest of the world.

There's a whole host of other reasons why our cultures are deemed "primitive", and to unpack this word in its entirety would require a book of its own. The point is that rather than actually examining the truth, the word "primitive" is so ingrained in European understandings of Africa that it presupposes any questions Europeans ask themselves about us. And it has real and continued effects.

Pre-Industrial

The moment I heard this word I thought about that Victorian theory of social evolutionism. Springing from Darwin's theory of evolution, it was believed that all societies fall upon a universal and unilineal evolutionist scheme. In the same way that species were found to evolve from simple to complex organisms, it was thought that cultures progressed from simple to complex states. Within this theory, different societies occupy different stages along this scheme and differ in terms of political organisation, kinship, religion, etc all developing towards one ideal civilised nation, such as those found in modern Europe. Clearly, the more "primitive" a culture was found to be, the further behind it was on this unilineal timeline.

Arguments such as this became the justification for racist colonial policies and anthropological practices. Complex civilisations were suppressed and destroyed because they were deemed backwards. There was and is this push to make African countries more European. An idea that all cultures naturally strive towards some neoliberal ideal, meaning that those that are dragging their feet can be given a shove in the right direction.

That few seem to be able to imagine a world outside of European norms is evidence of European cultural hegemony, brought about entirely because of the continent's colonial past and not because Europeans have somehow tapped into universal truths on how humans should organise themselves. There is no timeline; no reason why Africa's development should be plotted on a map that leads to Europe. In the context of an African continent that (but for colonialism) could have existed in any number of non-European forms, words like "pre-industrial" are unintelligible.

Savage

This word I find the most dangerous because it is, to me, incredibly dehumanising. Anything viewed as savage is immediately animalistic. It can therefore be treated as such.

Black African bodies are given no respect. With logic similar to that of proponents of the myth of black-on-black crime in countries like England and the United States, there's this idea that because Africans are always seen to be killing each other, our lives are worth less; it is perfectly reasonable not only for others to kill us but for our deaths to have less meaning.

So the genocides committed by various colonial powers across the African continent are ignored. Nevermind that those genocides are expressive of a savagery far more vicious than anything Europeans imagine of Africans. When we die, our bodies are broadcast across television screens, plastered on newspapers for shock value – except it doesn't shock anyone anymore. One of countless examples includes the media coverage of the terrorist attack on Garissa University in Kenya,[25] where un-blurred dead bodies were plastered on screens across the world. This is in direct contrast to the way in which the media dealt with white deaths in the Paris attacks carried out by ISIL that same year. Not only were warnings about the disturbing nature of the images presented before articles, the images of dead white bodies were pixelated out of respect.

To briefly go back to the journalist's comments mentioned above, I feel like it's this perceived savagery of all Africans that meant she failed to mention that there were victims (the Tutsis) to the Rwandan genocide. I doubt that she forgot that there were victims, but the murdered become irrelevant when the more common narrative focuses on those doing the murdering. It's easier to generalise Rwandans who are clearly at odds with each other (even without thinking) than is the case with European Bosnians who are not constantly subjected to this word and its connotations.

As we live, Africans are portrayed constantly in every form of media as war-hungry, cannibalistic, animalistic sub-humans. Incapable of being civilised, however one chooses to define that word. Westerners make jokes about our suffering because to them we are not human. Our pain isn't real. It can be mocked and then ignored. It frustrates me to no end when I try and talk to white friends about racist oppression and they pull out the "we-are-all-one-human-race" card, because clearly their Western peers would disagree. By their measure, I do not qualify.

******

Part of the reason these words have so much power is because they are

---

[25] https://www.bbc.co.uk/news/world-africa-32169080

repeated so often. Celebrated Nigerian author Chimamanda Ngozi Adichie perfectly captures this problem in her TED talk, "The Danger of a Single Story".[26] She exposes the Western tendency to treat the African continent as having one narrative, one fostered over generations to the point where in order to properly learn about Africa, one must first unlearn everything they had previously thought. In one quote she says it all: "Show people as one thing over and over again, and that's what they become."

Those three words have become Africa, but we are challenging this. To use a personal example, I tried to help found an African and Caribbean publishing house that sought to platform stories previously silenced and unheard. "Unrealistic" stories about Africans in the Diaspora coming to terms with their identity. Stories about Africans living lives that have nothing to do with poverty and/or war.

Beyond that young Africans are building new platforms for themselves on various forms of media to challenge misconceptions and coded language of Africans as primitive, pre-industrial, and savage. And so a domino effect is created. Refraining from the use of this language and defining ourselves forces others to challenge their perceptions, which in turn makes them less likely to use that language.

There can only be good in taking the obvious fact that language has meaning and applying it to the way that we collectively perceive others. It will take a lot of work to change people's views. But our first steps could simply concern the use of three words.

---

[26] Adichie, Chimamanda Ngozi, "The Danger of a Single Story." TedTalk, https://www.youtube.com/watch?v=D9Ihs241zeg

We Are Not Your Playthings

Lola Olufemi

This article was written in response to the commissioning of a personal diary by a white student entitled '10 Weeks in Kampala' published by a student newspaper at Cambridge.

There are many things to be said about exploring the world. It's natural for us to want to go out and have new experiences, to push ourselves by seeking out thrills and adventures, things that will test us. What irks me is that there are white middle class people who have the money, time and space to "discover" my homeland in ways that are not even afforded to me, someone from Nigeria. Acknowledgement is always the first step in breaking down practices and systems that contribute to the oppression and dehumanisation of other people, but it is not enough simply to recognise the privilege of being able to fly to an African country and volunteer, or being white in Africa.

There is nothing new, radical or interesting about going to a continent that your ancestors pillaged and destroyed, all the while enslaving its inhabitants, and then writing about how you feel like an outsider for the first time. Colonised countries are not an emotional playground. They are not there to teach you anything about yourself or to reveal how race operates or to remind you that you are lucky. You don't get to use colonised countries and people as a means of self-discovery. You don't get to up and decide that you're going to move to Kampala because those people are in need of your services. Not only does that show a complete and utter disregard for colonial history, using other human beings to enrich your life and experiences is also violently voyeuristic. It is dangerous to explore the world, especially as a white person, with the intention of "doing good" without first examining the reasons why you think that is necessary.

No doubt, the media has painted an image of Africa so unlike your reality that you might feel compelled to go and help. Yes, poverty exists in Africa, like it exists in the UK. But, to steal the words of Chimamanda Ngozi Adichie, Africa is not a single story; she is multifaceted, and so are her people. Consider that when you go to Africa – a continent so heavily theorised by white media and white academics – and then write about how you are scammed, touched, hollered at, you contribute to a global understanding of Africans as scary and savage. Consider that when you marvel at the use of witchcraft and native rituals, you reaffirm a perception of Africa as backward. Consider that, by centering yourself in discussions about an Africa that is suffering for the large part because of the continent you represent, you add nothing of value to broader discourse. There is nothing inherently transformative about writing about your social and political experiences if you belong to a dominant group. History is full of your experiences. Consider that going to Africa – or, indeed, any of the former colonies – as a middle class white person might do more harm than good.

We must start looking past dominant narratives that tell us that Africa is in need of our help. It shows an astounding level of entitlement to think that you, on your gap year or your three weeks abroad "exploring", are going to do anything meaningful or long lasting to help the communities that you fetishize. If your aim is to help someone, why is volunteering at your local food bank not enough? Why is flying halfway around the world and infiltrating a culture that you won't fully understand a better option? Because your local food bank isn't exotic. You can't watch the sun rise and fall over Hackney in the same way you can over Kampala.

At the very least, there must be a recognition of the inward-looking desires that drive a large majority of white middle class people into voluntourism. That Africa exists to teach you something new about yourself or make you feel good is evidence of dehumanisation.

Prefacing an article on being white in Africa with an acknowledgement of colonial history and then insisting on writing about your experience shows that you haven't fully engaged with it, as if your "experience" of Africa, your "experience" of India in any way nullifies the violent colonial structures that you are reproducing. Africa and Africans are not an aesthetic that you can get to pull on and off; they are not your cover photos or props to counteract the guilt you might feel for being middle class. If ever the White Gaze revealed itself, it's in this constant need to "tell others" about how beautiful colonised countries are, how humble and happy the people are despite how little they have. The contrast between the state of your lives and theirs is not a tool for your emotional exploitation.

This is not a call to end Western aid. This is about what it means to see your homeland constantly used to fulfil the desires of Westerners. This is about what it feels like to be in conversations with white people who tell you that, "Ugandans are like this" or "the Vietnamese are like this" after spending no more than two months there. This is about ownership of narratives that do not belong to white people. Africa is in debt to the countries that stole from her; Europe must bear the brunt of the responsibility for her underdevelopment. Acknowledging that in an article where you then go on to reaffirm stereotypes and treat formerly colonised land as the "great unknown" is not enough. If you had actually engaged with that idea at all or given it a second thought, you might have decided to call your trip off. You might have decided to seriously interrogate your intentions when going abroad. You might have considered that it is not "your experience" that is most at stake.

Palatability

Waithera Sebatindira

After describing herself as a radical feminist, a friend of mine suggested I'd be better at working "within the system". I silently fumed as she spoke because it struck a nerve. Whenever I've led workshops on intersectional feminism, white women have come up to me afterwards and complimented me on how calmly or eloquently I spoke. Very few of the people I've met at Cambridge have seen me angry. Received Pronunciation is the shape of my accent. I am palatable.

This isn't an inherently bad thing. I've had to learn how to strategically swallow my anger, and as a result there are people I've reached who I would otherwise have alienated. I'm good at compartmentalising. I take the rage I feel when, for example, I encounter dog-whistle politics in the media. I place it into a box, which I shut. I break down the racism/sexism/misogynoir for the benefit of people who "don't get what the big deal is".[27] If they've genuinely come to listen, then sometimes their eyes will widen, they'll understand, and they'll thank me for explaining it to them so logically. Most do not. Regardless, I unpack the rage alone.

That I can almost automatically set aside my emotions in political spaces isn't deliberate. I think it's a self-defence mechanism; a way of getting around the double-burden of simultaneously experiencing misogynoir and educating my oppressor on it. It makes what I say easy

---

[27] 'Misogynoir' was coined by queer black feminist Moya Bailey, who created the term to address misogyny directed toward black women in American visual and popular culture.

to swallow. Makes me palatable. And I hate it.

I'm a firm believer in the necessity of anger in liberation politics. I maintain that it's the difference between those who talk about injustice and those who do something about it. I reject arguments that black women who speak passionately also speak irrationally and, therefore, can be ignored. I want to stick in people's throats because ultimately the truths I want to share are uncomfortable. Yet it's too easy for me to set anger aside, soften my voice to communicate my experiences to those who do not share them.

When my feminist friend said I'd be good "in the system", she meant at my new job as Women's Officer for the students' union.[28] It's true that it's a job that requires diplomacy and engagement. I'm excited by that. But it's also a radical role, born of the frustrations of women forced to tackle the university's 784-year-old legacy of patriarchal domination alongside their degree. These women said "enough" and the university was forced to listen. If I'm to continue their work, I need my anger to do the role justice.

What worries me is that there have been times when I've been too good at thinking dispassionately about my own liberation. I've become a cynic. Maybe I burned myself out, but now, when faced with certain issues, I think about what is realistic before I think about what is right. Being conscious of it and correcting myself doesn't feel like enough. There are days when I look at Cambridge as an institution and I wonder "Should we bother?" This institution surely cannot be decolonised. Formal equality is the most it can manage. I've looked for breaches and loopholes and none have been found.

There are a number of methods I use to remind myself to remain radical. But the most important is shaped by the memory of my ancestors. What they endured, what they could never have imagined enduring, and what they deserve. I don't know their individual stories.

---

[28] 'As Students' Union Women's Officer I was elected for a full-time, one-year sabbatical role representing the interests of women and non-binary students at the University. Broadly, this involved lobbying the university and helping students organise feminist campaigns.

I know very little about my family line. What I can imagine, though, is what they'd want the world to look like today.

I often think about my favourite Nayyirah Waheed poem titled '*sight*':

> my ancestors made sure
> i was born
> the colour of their
> eyes [29]

And when I do I'm also reminded of one of the final lines in '*Still I Rise*': "I am the dream and the hope of the slave." [30]

I can imagine what that hope looks like. Not undue deference, but action. When I read that poem I remember that we deserve no less than to be totally liberated right now, this instant. Not when it's deemed convenient. I fight harder knowing that I shouldn't have to ask for the things that I'm forced to ask for nonetheless. I like the idea of my ancestors seeing the new world through me and nodding with approval. More importantly, I see that, although too little change will come about over the course of our lives, I can be a small part of the legacy that will ultimately create a world of which I can be proud. Just as the fact that I could even attend Cambridge is entirely down to people who fought urgent, painful battles before me.

Beyond becoming unpalatable to whiteness, there's the strange reality that I can be unpalatable to black people, too – even while discussing liberation. I've encountered many black people who would deny me my blackness on the basis of their own self-abasing and limited conceptions of it. It took awhile for me to appreciate that I can define my blackness for myself. Since I began finding the words to define my own experience - as a black woman specifically, and human being more

[29] waheed, n.2013. sight. In: n. waheed. 2013. salt. CreateSpace Independent Publishing Platform. p. 210.

[30] Angelou, M, "Still I Rise." 1978. Poetry Foundation. [online] Available at: https://www.poetryfoundation.org/poems/46446/still-i-rise

generally - I've stopped trying to limit myself by trying to find a language that's deemed acceptable by every black person I encounter. I recognise my blackness, and that's enough. It's the product of a variety of different black cultures. It remains stubbornly undefined, and it is mine alone.

There. Now I remember that there is a time and a place for tact, but no longer for palatability. Liberation should be threatening because it comes to destroy and build anew. I want the thought of it to leave a bad taste in your mouth.

PART THREE:
Radical Self-Love

Our existence is our act of resistance against the world built
against us.

-

looking in the mirror
i think of you and wonder how the earth has not yet teetered
off its axis. i see you and think i must be seeing things because
the flowers are in bloom
even if the leaves reached back to their roots
long ago. it's like i'm drowning in a shallow pool,
except my lungs are filled not with water but grit.
you are alive and your breaths are deep and
that is so much more than enough.

-Jun Pang

Learning to Stop Saying 'Sorry'

Suhaiymah Manzoor-Khan

My first attempt to do something with my revitalized anger, to do something with my frustration at those around me who denied me my fullest existence, was to write something. Perhaps it wasn't shouting, but at this stage anything was better than silence. It marked a new start. The start of proclaiming my difference, the start of no longer hiding, and the start of writing becoming a source of comfort and liberation. It was me gasping for air in that sea of mayonnaisey white and saying 'I refuse to be drowned out. You will see me'. I remember it clearly; it was a lengthy Facebook post.

I wrote about how tired I was of being talked over, how tired I was of being assumed and patronised. I wrote about my hijab.

"At its bare bones, the headscarf, or hijab as it is often called, is a piece of cloth (the niqab,[31] although I do not wear it, is only another aspect of this). However, like most things, it gains significance through the meanings we give it. When I first chose to wear the hijab at age fourteen the reasons had to do with my surge of interest in the religion I had been brought up in: a desire to feel pious, to feel a sense of belonging, and to convey in a symbol my belief in God. However, six years down the line my reasons have evolved and accumulated and this piece of cloth is now also a symbol of my feminism, of anti-capitalism, anti-imperialism and of my values and beliefs about the world.

It concerns me that some feminists are only just realising the feeling of

---

[31] A garment of cloth that covers the face, worn by some Muslim women.

empowerment that many women who wear the hijab gain from it. In the same way feminists advocate that women should be free to wear what they want and that their bodies are their own to make choices about, when I put on my hijab in the morning I too am making these decisions. I am affirming, in my own way, that this body is mine to cover if I so wish and that I above anyone else am in control of its fabulous entirety. This triangle of cloth, is to me, a symbol against objectification. A symbol of choice and a symbol that I desire complete control of the sexualisation of my own body. I refuse to meet the standards placed upon me (contradictory standards no woman can ever meet, by the way).

To me my headscarf represents my belief and hope that all people should be respected for who they are, rather than what they look like. A hope that we can live in a world where women wear whatever they want without fear; that the rape-culture of victim-blaming – women being told how to dress to protect themselves – can be destroyed; that a culture of women being bodies first and foremost – think page 3 and how normalised this is – can be undone, and that someday we will not judge books by their covers.

Choosing to cover rather than uncover is not a fear of my sexuality; it is not fear of men; it is not an internalised inferiority-complex; not a way to police my body – it is a gesture which allows me to control my own body, remember Allah, and assert myself. Especially when I am telling you so myself; especially in a place where there are no laws forcing me to wear it; especially when I keep it on despite an increase in Islamophobic attacks against visibly Muslim women. Why are our voices not enough then? Why are our choices deemed false consciousness?

A woman who chooses to uncover would probably use similar arguments: that her body is her own, that she refuses to be policed, that she should not be objectified or sexualised just because she has skin showing. The hijab, in my mind, is a way of expressing a similar belief. Why is uncovering necessarily more empowering than covering? Can women not do what they feel most comfortable with? Must we glorify one mode of empowerment above another? Whose definitions get priority and why?

In these choices I also feel I am rejecting the constraints society has set for me

My hijab reflects my views on capitalism and consumerism. This piece of cloth reveals my refusal to look the way advertisers say I should; my refusal to buy into patriarchal media representations of human happiness. My scarf represents me placing my Islamic spiritual satisfaction above worldly goods and consumerism. To me, it embodies my rejection of the harmful, capitalistic, unsustainable, anti-women, commodified society we live in today, and symbolises my hope for tomorrow.

But, once again, let me emphasise that it is just a piece of cloth — just as hair spray is a chain of molecules and a tattoo is some ink. The meaning I give to the hijab is my own alone, it derives from my beliefs about the world I live in, and the way I see myself in it. It is a choice just like any other that people make every day. Though important to me and in my relationship with God, it really ought not to affect anyone else. And yet, because it is the symbol of a religion I am part of, I am burdened with the responsibility of representing 'Islam' in all I do. And it is because of this responsibility that we women who choose to wear hijabs are plagued like any minority group in having to prove our worth and our intelligence and value, before our choice will be fully respected and recognised."

Although my views on this topic have grown more nuanced and complicated since then[32] (and I now question why I should ever have felt the pressure to answer this question posed by voyeuristic eyes at all; and I also spend much more of my time speaking publicly about all the meanings given by others to Muslim women's clothes and understand the function of such focus much better having researched, spoken and written on it widely), this was the start of something. A small ripple - an exciting ripple.

The feedback I got surprised me. People wanted to talk about it. They wanted to hear more. I went to the college cafe and people acknowledged and referred to what I had written. The fear I had learnt to nurture around what made me stand out was shattered. In realising

---

[32] There is so much more that could and should be said on this topic regarding translation, word meaning, interpretation, intention and context - however, this is what I wrote at the time so I leave it here in good faith that it is understood as a product of my thinking at the time.

I had stood out all along and I could neither meet people's expectations of a Muslim woman of Pakistani heritage, nor change them, I simply began to be me regardless.

Bringing my Islamic identity to the fore was liberating. It was often my identification as a Muslim – symbolised through the hijab – that had been made a hurdle for me. Or, I should say, a hurdle for others. It was my Muslim identity which impacted understandings of my gender, my Muslim identity which prevented me fitting 'normal' student tropes; my Muslim identity which caused most awkwardness. In a context wherein Islam, 'The War On Terror', Muslim women, 'The Middle East', 'Fundamentalism', 'Terrorism' and 'Extremism' were all buzzwords absorbed into general discourse, being visibly Muslim at Cambridge had been exhausting. I was always second-guessing what people thought of what I did, always feeling the need to defend, always getting those awkward glances when any remote reference to Islam was made. Addressing my 'Muslim-ness' myself, and jumping immediately to the visual symbol of it, knocked down an invisible wall. It relaxed me, made me more at home and made me realise it was not my faith or myself that were to blame, but society's treatment of those things. My fear of standing out came not from within, but was imposed from without.

Of course, with many people – and all the people who never saw the Facebook post – little changed. Still, from the reactions that I did get, it signalled to me that perhaps writing was a medium through which I could communicate and become someone fierce, someone who would defend herself and someone who could explain herself. Later on I would reject the notion that I should defend or explain myself; but the feeling of finally being in control that came with dictating the terms on which people immediately judged me was a powerful moment. I began to make writing a compulsory part of my experience at Cambridge. Writing for myself, mainly, but sometimes things I'd share I kept diaries, wrote poems, articles, thoughts; wrote on sadness, anger, excitement, joy. This was a new realm for me. A realm where, alone with my thoughts, I could realise things, explore things and slowly

I could validate and understand the feelings that would otherwise be erased in the white outside world.

In many ways, writing about feeling helped me to feel. Writing to validate myself was a form of self-care: a listening to my own voice when nobody else would. I often found that by the end of a page of writing I had discovered something new about myself, something I had not been able to articulate the day before. In times when my mental health was bad – something absolutely brought about by the nature of Cambridge and its institutional pressures, racism and exclusionary norms – writing became a solace and a friend. It was a way to accept and grow myself at times of alienation and anger – after so long of hiding, hurting, pretending and still being locked out, it was a way to be me without being afraid. Writing allowed me to unapologetically make room for, rather than crush, my brownness, my gender and my Islam.

The more I wrote and the more I shared what I wrote, the braver I became. I took Audre Lorde's words to heart and realised that I had little to lose: *'Your silences will not protect you… They will interrupt you, put you down and suggest it's personal. And the world won't end. And the speaking will get easier and easier. And you will find you have fallen in love with your own vision, which you may never have realized you had… And at last you'll know with surpassing certainty that only one thing is more frightening than speaking your truth. And that is not speaking.'* [33]

I became unapologetic. If my conversations made people uncomfortable, I would simply keep talking. If my exposing oppressions and injustice troubled them it said more about them than me. In this renewed voice and life, I found there came an understanding that the way I was and the way people expected me to be would never reconcile.

I stopped berating myself over the fact people constantly said I didn't

---

[33] Audre Lorde, 'The Transformation of Silence into Language and Action' in Sister Outsider, 1984.

'sound like' I was from Yorkshire. Well, I told myself, they wouldn't either if they had been encouraged to adapt to a system wherein sounding like a middle-class white woman is more likely to get you a place at Cambridge than sounding like a Yorkshire-Pakistani. I sounded too posh to be from Yorkshire, and I didn't sound Asian enough to be Asian; I acted too white, I acted too Muslim; there was no winning.

I remember the moment my friends turned to me, shocked, upon hearing I had never had a Yorkshire Pudding. How could I, a Yorkshire lass, not have had a Yorkshire pudding? The simultaneity of their blindness and the suffocation of their forcefulness made me realise that I never was a 'Yorkshire lass'. I lived in Leeds and visited my grandparents weekly in Bradford, sure, but my dinners were *roti-boti, salan, gosht, daal, chaval* and *aloo-parahta*. I was a third-generation Pakistani Muslim girl who grew up in Yorkshire. I never fit the romanticised English imaginings of working-class, down-the-pub, Yorkshire-pudding, ee-by-gum, masculine, white, Yorkshire. But by the same token, I never fit the orientalist, ill-informed, racist and homogenous imaginings of a South Asian Muslim woman. There was no winning. Both and all doors were shut. I sprawled across their boxes, messy and confusing.

This is the same reality that belongs to many third-generation migrant children. We own the world of the margins – the part of the brain that understands multiple languages; the clothing that reflects our culture in new ways; and the ground that is profoundly ours despite barriers all around. We are not entirely part of the migrant community, yet we remain excluded from 'Britishness' defined narrowly as whiteness.[34] We are uniquely free, but sometimes it hurts too. It hurts that I know the coloniser's tongue better than my own, and yet for that I am deemed inauthentically brown. Why is it that I had to forget the language that birthed me to access racist institutions?

---

[34] See Louise Casey, *A Review into opportunity and integration*, December 2016

On the other hand, language is not the key to my heritage. I know when I go to my grandparents' home I am profoundly *theirs*. There can be no inauthenticity when 'authenticity' itself is a sham of ill-informed generalisations. Yet, at times it does pain me to think I've learnt more about Indian and Pakistani history and regional/local norms through books and academic research than I have through real life. Paradoxically, that is the price I have paid to access another culture, too. Being an outsider in *both* worlds is where the pain comes in.

I am simultaneously brown, Muslim, woman, and Yorkshire. But these labels confine and they confuse. I am not each of these things. I am all of these things and none of them. I am a simultaneity of things, but with them I am one. When people choose to box and categorise, they limit my personhood. They slice me into understandable chunks that make no sense to me. So when I decided to be unapologetically me, I meant the whole of me, with space to accept I may change and grow. There were no more explanations, no more justifications and no more focusing on helpful labels that could be used to pack me neatly away.

The following is a poem I wrote during my second year at Cambridge after a conversation with one of my History supervisors at a formal hall meal.

Didn't You Know?

didn't you know
white men invented everything

his rotting breath spills into my side of the room
as he
explains to me
my humanity

he extracts my limbs from his teeth
and deconstructs me on the table
amidst cheeses I can't pronounce
as if i too can be consumed
and finished off in the next round

he deconstructs and dissects
the same way they did so many continents
probably on tables just like this

but didn't i know white men invented everything
they didn't deconstruct
they constructed
continents wouldn't exist without their toilet paper touch

i am not there

i am never there

i am not real outside of his gorged and purpling lips

should i thank him then
for mentioning me
for legitimising my existence

he leans forward
as he does another white man comes into view
a portrait just above his head
a mirror image minus several hundred years

you mustn't talk only about race
he tells me
you have to consider gender, too

i don't know what to say in response
he wants a back-pat for having just invented me
for just having created categories
to fit my existence into

but his invention of me is my undoing
i cannot now exist outside his mind
i am boxed
i am trapped
i am being contained

contained in the same way that borders are just pen
marks on paper
but also they are pain

and in boxing me
he splits me
segments me
and takes my voice

it used to be a joke that i never finished my sentences
that i was always ready to be talked over
ready to be cut off

it used to be a joke that there was silence
because nobody listens to silence

he tells me i am abstract
not one thing but a series of disjointed reports
not real just skin

didn't you know white men invented everything
the boxes i am in are not my own
and the words of this poem are the only ones i know
but not the ones i chose to learn

didn't you know white men invented everything
i look in the mirror and ask if i really know me
if anyone does
because whose performance am i
in what cage do i belong

i cannot talk only about race
but i cannot talk of gender too
for i am not two
things
i am one

but didn't i know white men invented everything
the art of talking
the art of being one

they will lie to you
that you cannot exist outside their mouths
and thus you must come in bitesize chunks
palatable

but he does not know that i have invented him
I have invented him not because i need him
only to make a point

but he
he cannot forsake me
for to forsake me
is to forsake part of his white self that is so visible he
thinks it invisible
that he thinks race and gender apply only to me
weapons in his hands
they dissolve in mine

i am not there
it is he who is
he invents me so he can breathe
he imagines me so i cannot

sometimes a poem is not enough because it is only
words
and sometimes a poem is too much because it is
words
but it's somewhere to exist
outside their mouths

A Poem about Queerness

"You only have to let the soft animal of your body love what it loves."
- Mary Oliver

I don't know which form this should take,
maybe a story, song or poem, something to quell doubt.
Short story... lips touch, momentary peace, then the world invades.
men jeer
you're constantly aware of everything that could be lost.
Loss taunts you, gain dances on your skin.
You begin to question that kiss, the strength of that look, the smell of her hair.
Something stops you from telling yourself back to you.
When you can, make it memorable, like it is to the people who kill you for it.
There will come a time for parents, the natural order and rationality - but now,
for now, breathe in all of her, bite tongues, touch skin, without thinking.
.

your mother will learn to love you again,
she must.

-A Fly Girl

Crossing Borders and Self-Love
Waithera Sebatindira

Education may be the great equaliser, but not all educational institutions are created equal. Going to a university like Cambridge makes this all the more clear.

The university is clearly marked out by borders. Even on a geographical level, there is a sharp difference between the areas of the town enriched by the presence of the university and those occupied by its less wealthy permanent residents. The borders I'll focus on here, though, are those that demarcate Cambridge University as, among other things, a place of privilege, imperialist conceptions of intellect, and, most importantly, hegemonic whiteness.

This wouldn't be much of an issue if not for the fact that Cambridge is also ranked as one of the best universities in the world. Oxbridge provide an excellent education, one that is genuinely unparalleled by any other university in the UK. It should be the number one destination for any ambitious, hard-working student, and, for a lot of them, it is.

But there are also too many who, despite being perfectly capable, don't apply. Faced with a choice between a great but isolating education, and a slightly less respected degree achieved around people to whom they can relate, they choose the latter. Beyond them there are young people who feel that most, if not all, universities don't exist for people like them.

I'll state here that while imperialistic thinking is an inherently bad thing, the detrimental consequences of Cambridge's privilege and hegemonic whiteness must be explained. The privilege I'm referring to is that associated with the kind of old money at the university's foundation. The old, gorgeous buildings, the robes, the Latin prayers. In England, regular engagement with this world is deemed a luxury only accessible to an extremely wealthy few. But it's also a part of the history of all English people, and it's important that Cambridge is able to open up that world to more people; ostensibly anyone who's deemed worthy by its fairly arbitrary standards.

The problem is that privilege of every kind is inherently exclusive. Those spaces were created with the intention that only a certain, small group of people would be able to enjoy them. While the white middle-class seems to have built up an entitlement to that privilege over the years, anecdotal evidence has suggested to me that black Britons and the black working-class in particular still find that it's a space that doesn't belong to them. It seems that the kind of privilege heavily associated with Cambridge is also robbing some Britons (and international students) of the sense of entitlement to the university they might otherwise have had by virtue of their academic ability. While the solution obviously isn't necessarily to get rid of all of Cambridge's traditions, the alienating effects of this privilege clearly need to be countered.

This detrimental consequence of privilege is exacerbated by the issue of hegemonic whiteness, a concept best explained by American sociologist Amanda Lewis in her 2004 paper ""What Group?" Studying Whites and Whiteness in the Era of "Color-Blindness""[35]

"For an ideology to gain hegemony it must do more than enable people to make sense of their lives; it must successfully naturalize the status quo. In naturalizing and legitimating the present state of things, ideologies tend to support certain interests and to subvert others... Ideologies become hegemonic to the extent that they enable people to understand and to accept their positions within a stratified society. They gain consent from those

---

[35] Lewis, A E. (2004) ""What Group?" Studying Whites and Whiteness in the Era of "Color-Blindness"", Sociological Theory, 22(4), pp. 623–646.

on various rungs of the social ladder to a system that secures the positions of both the dominated and the dominating.
(Hall 1986; Gramsci 1971).[36]

Hegemonic whiteness then would be that "configuration of [racial] practice which embodies the currently accepted answer to the problem of the legitimacy of [white supremacy]" and that secures the dominant position of whites (Connell 1995:77)..."[37]

In the context of Cambridge (and in specific reference to black students), hegemonic whiteness expresses itself in the fact that there are too few non-white students and little critical evaluation of why that's the case. It's a fact that's simply been accepted due either to the misguided belief that people of colour are less academically able (or inclined) than white people, or an apathetic awareness of structural inequalities that don't exist in our favour. It's also evidenced by the Eurocentric curriculum and the erasure of PoC in popular discourse surrounding Cambridge. While it makes sense for whiteness to be the norm at a university where over 70%[37] of the students are white, whiteness dominates in a way that prevents the meaningful introduction of necessary non-white influences into the culture and curriculum.

This presents an obvious problem in terms of access, as black people are justified in rejecting the prospect of three years of isolation at a place where they cannot see themselves for the sake of a degree. No one should have to ignore a fundamental aspect of their identity to succeed in an educational institution. Yet in not applying, many black people are also potentially shutting themselves out of opportunities for greater economic self-sufficiency and material (albeit often necessary) gain. This is why it's so important for those of us who do cross the borders into spaces like Cambridge to find ways to break them.

---

[36] Gramsci, Antonio, Quintin Hoare, and Geoffry N. Smith. Selections from the Prison Notebooks.

[37] https://www.equality.admin.cam.ac.uk/files/information_report_2015-16_final.pdf

It's worth noting here that "hegemonic whiteness is not a quality inherent to individual whites but is a collective social force that shapes their lives just as it shapes the lives of racial minorities."[38] Moreover, it's "also something people may well have only partial access to and that regularly is contested. For example, colloquial references to blacks "acting white" and to whites behaving as "wiggers"[39] all are examples of people partially crossing borders in and out of hegemonic whiteness with varying degrees of reward or penalty."[40] People of colour can perform and even identify with hegemonic whiteness (e.g. by embracing certain cultural practices or defending institutional practices). The problem remains that those who don't embrace hegemonic whiteness in a place like Cambridge risk suffering the consequences, be it a rejected essay style or an alternative reading list that might provide a more rounded education, but fails to prepare one for their exams. On a non-academic level, rejecting white hegemony might also lead to alienation from the majority of the student body.

Knowing what it is that the borders of Cambridge protect makes knowing how to break them easier. In fact, knowing this also means being aware that the crossing and breaking of those borders must be a radical act. And when I say "radical" I refer to its Latin etymology, meaning 'forming the root'. That is, in order to break borders one must get to the root of their existence and pull it out, rather than trying to bring about change through more tangential measures.

I've been very lucky in my life that my mum has had a job that allowed her to send me to private schools and then on to Cambridge. I've always assumed that using this privilege for good involved crossing borders into spaces that were historically not open to black people, thereby pulling other black people up as I went along. But the methods I had in mind were not radical enough.

---

[38] Lewis, 2004.
[39] A dated term used to describe white people who try to emulate cultural behaviour attributed to black people.
[40] Lewis, 2004.

I used to have a set process in mind:

1) Through discipline and hard work, enter spaces (such as Cambridge) that don't historically belong to you.
2) Learn what white people in those spaces value and learn how to excel in their culture through mimicry and assimilation.
3) At some point, go back to the border and teach younger black people how to mimic white people so they can make their way into and through these spaces even faster than you did.

I essentially felt like it was my job to give black people the cheat codes to life among successful white people. That was how one broke borders. Then we'd flood these spaces with assimilated black folk and white people would have to accept that whatever they could do, we could do, too. The only thing standing in our way was black people who didn't see it as their responsibility to teach the next generation how to succeed.

This approach is good to the extent that it can introduce white people in places like Cambridge to the diversity of black experiences: we can be anything from Lady Leshurr[41] to David Lammy[42]. I also understand that it's the pragmatic approach. It's easier to climb the social ladder than it is to deconstruct it. Harder to change a culture than to work within it. However, all this realistically does is serve to maintain borders rather than break them.

By assimilating into white hegemony anywhere, one reinforces it as a good thing, thus making it more difficult for other black people to enter into and benefit from spaces like Cambridge. It changes nothing and merely allows the status quo to continue. For one thing, it's been my experience that when exposed to me, finding that I don't fit into their conception of blackness, many white people have merely made

---

[41] A famous grime artist.
[42] A prominent and vocal Member of Parliament for the UK Labour Party.

me an exception to their stereotype, rather than actually tackling their prejudices. Moreover, "breaking borders" by encouraging others to assimilate into white hegemony won't lead to the liberation of all black people – just those who are willing to assimilate. On a more abstract level, our instinct when we come across an instance of white supremacy shouldn't be to change ourselves to fit into it. It should be to destroy it.

Most importantly, I feel like this approach evinces a lack of black self-love. We shouldn't be so willing to shed aspects of our identity and replace it with what's valued under white hegemony. Not only should we be proud of our identities, but we should also want to see our blackness in spaces like Cambridge. We should use our heritage to shape these institutions rather than hide it like some shameful secret and, worse, encourage others to do the same.

It's not enough to make black people subscribe to certain cultural values while ignoring their own. If we want to break borders and genuinely draw more black people in, we should be able to see ourselves at Cambridge. Not just literally (by improving numbers), but at an institutional level as well. We should question reading lists that only have white authors, modules that trivialise and "other" non-European work, history, and culture. We should grow our cultural societies and try and force them into mainstream Cambridge culture. This is what we tried to do with FLY in 2015 by increasing its presence in the university through introducing the ideas of women of colour to the rest of the student body.

We should write our own stories about our time in places like Cambridge to complement the single story already told. The story that's found in books like *Brideshead Revisited*[43] and, more recently, on Caroline Calloway's Instagram account[44] –of white people struggling and celebrating amidst privilege – is valid; as true as mine or anyone

---

[43] Waugh, E. (1981). *Brideshead revisited: the sacred and profane memories of Captain Charles Ryder*, Harmondsworth, Penguin.
[44] https://thetab.com/uk/cambridge/2015/02/01/tab-meets-caroline-calloway-45726)

else's. But we need more people to share the real diversity of experiences that take place in Cambridge, too.

If we truly love our blackness, we'll see the value it can add to an already world-class education and want to share it as much as possible. And there are already people who do, to quote a friend, "incorporate their uniqueness" into their work. Bringing their blackness into their supervisions and exploring various aspects of it with their supervisors. This should be done as much as possible.

The reasons for why anyone might not love their blackness are both obvious and complex. Hegemonic whiteness extends far beyond Cambridge to the rest of the world. Two extracts from bell hooks' book 'Black Looks' cover the reasons why quite well for me:

"A culture of domination demands of all its citizens self-negation. The more marginalised, the more intense the demand. Since black people, especially the underclass, are bombarded by messages that we have no value, are worthless, it is no wonder that we fall prey to nihilistic despair..."

"As long as black folks are taught that the only way we can gain any degree of economic self-sufficiency or be materially privileged is by first rejecting blackness, our history and culture, then there will always be a crisis in black identity."[45]

Self-love while black can therefore be an exceptionally difficult thing. We're all taught, regardless of race or background, to value whiteness above everything else. Be it through classical music, white literature, or the remnants of the Greek and Roman Empires, we're taught that whiteness changed the world while the rest of us watched. It's no wonder, then, that when so many of us cross the border into a space from where pioneers and leaders are said to originate, we accept the whiteness of that space and expect other black people to follow suit.

But self-love is essential if we are to break the borders to places like Cambridge. When black people can see that they'll be valued

---

[45] hooks, b. (1992). *Black looks: race and representation.* Boston. MA, South End Press.

in these spaces – that they won't have to sacrifice any part of themselves – then those borders will finally be broken. We must teach Cambridge how to love blackness as much as we do. We must break down its hegemonic whiteness as much as is possible to make blackness a valued part of the culture. Not only will that benefit prospective applicants who will know they'll be accepted, but it could also enrich the education that the university provides by drawing on the good that blackness can bring.

It is, of course, impossible to produce a blanket definition of "blackness". As a Kenyan who didn't really identify as black until mid-adolescence, it's hard to know what's meant by the term and what it claims to represent. But I think the answer is both personal and obvious to a black reader from any part of the world who encounters this idea of "blackness". Beyond the tropes, there is cultural meaning in blackness. My mind will likely change on the subject, but I think it's safe to say, for now, that blackness means whatever it means to whichever black person tries to define it as they apply it to themselves, their families, their history (especially in relation to other races), social justice, and the work of other black people which they consume or of which they are aware.

On a final note, it is worth noting that part of the reason it is so difficult to see how we have to deconstruct white hegemony in order to break borders is because crossing borders is very closely tied to the capitalist dream. It's clear that within a capitalist framework success and equality are primarily measured in accordance with how much money one is allowed to earn, how much power a person is allowed to hold. So because a minority of black people increasingly have access to both money and power, it's easy to think that borders don't need to be broken by changing the culture. The culture appears to already accept us.

However, there are other ways in which to measure equality which are less superficial and, in my opinion, more telling: how your colleagues treat you; your treatment by the state; the way you're represented in the media; the way people talk about your success; whether your people's history is taught in classrooms; whether the work that your people have produced is respected; and, most importantly, whether you're really at peace where you are. These things become important when you value your blackness (as well as your general well-being) as much as you value success. Understanding that these factors are important leads us to see that to actually break borders we need to do more than mimic whiteness and buy into its hegemony.

It's easier in theory than in reality to practice the kind of radical self-love required to abolish borders. To be both unapologetically black and wildly successful. But we should try, otherwise we're destined to lose ourselves even as we try and do better for ourselves. We can have it all. We should.

On Cambridge and Being Grateful
Lola Olufemi

"Cambridge was a joy. Tediously." - Zadie Smith[46]

When Zadie Smith was interviewed at the English Faculty in 2015, she read one of her short stories and answered some questions. She spoke about how grateful she was to Cambridge for what it taught her and the career that it had allowed. It got me thinking about what it means to be grateful to an institution that was not built for you. Working class students of colour feel this most acutely; elite institutions are framed as the end goal, a marker of true success and this often leaves no space to express dissatisfaction, resentment, anger. Their criticisms are silenced because for some, getting to Cambridge nullifies all other structural oppression. This kind of thinking dictates that we must be in a constant state of gratitude to the institution; worship its systems and academics or else the 'chance' they have taken on us is lost somehow. Students of colour are constantly framed as infiltrators; people who do not really belong to the space.

Cambridge has taught me many things: how to punctuate sentences correctly, the art of analysis, the meaning of 'hendiadys,"[47] it has given me access to obscure journals and articles that I would never have read otherwise. It introduced me to young artists and activists who challenged my thinking in ways that have left indelible marks. I've met intelligent, radical women and non-binary people here and been given

---

[46] 'Learning Curve,' an Interview with Zadie Smith by Aida Edemariam in *The Guardian*, https://www.theguardian.com/books/2005/sep/03/fiction-zadiesmith
[47] The expression of a single idea by two words connected with 'and', e.g. nice and warm, when one could be used to modify the other, as in nicely warm.

opportunities that would not have happened at another university. What struck me being here is the sense of importance that people ascribe to their beliefs and activities because of the pervasive myth that we are the best the country has to offer. "That person is going to be influential one day" is a ridiculous and scarily accurate mantra that is repeated often. But when the same faces from the same private schools, like the ones that adorn the walls of our dining halls make it here at the expense of all others, and if around 0.5% of the undergraduate population is black, we cannot claim that Cambridge as it stands holds the 'most intelligent' people in the country. The assertion is ridiculous: the elitist idea that a single institution could harbour the country's potential must be done away with. The answer is not merely inclusion, as if the right number of black faces changes anything. The answer is to remain cognisant of the matrix of power relations and discourses that have created a hierarchical and deeply unequal education system in the first place.

Short of tearing the institution to the ground and starting again, all those engaged in resistance work can do is work in and outside of the institution to transform it. We must use its resources against it and remain critical of the experiences of the most marginalised and how the institution silences their dissent. But the changes that we wish for cannot happen without an acknowledgment that there is a problem, and herein lies the problem.

Sometimes students of colour get the sense that people want them to shut up and be grateful. Cambridge will drag you out as their token minority, their "success story", as evidence of their "state school intake" but in the process, demand that you be quiet about the reality of your experiences whilst you are here. This puts you in a strange position. You're forced to choose between having to "package" your rage and pleas for transformation in a way that will "get white men on side" and raising a holy middle finger to an institution that values only certain parts of you.

Case in point, colleges and faculties will ask students of colour to lead access tours, put us on the front of their prospectus, ask us to write positive testimonials, but refuse to do anything about the eurocentric male-dominated curriculum. Tutors will shrug and sigh and say, "isn't it a shame, that's just the way it is, we're very traditional here" and your frustration will know no bounds. You will try and vocalise how it feels to be interrogated by a porter, assumed a foreigner, walk into a hall of white faces or experience a microaggression to your white friends, and they will stare back at you perplexed. Rational dude-bros or trademark liberals will ask that you agitate for change more politely; that you try not to hurt the feelings of white men in demanding that your humanity is recognised and, better yet, protected. On top of this, we are expected to perform deference; "aren't we so *lucky* to be here?"

It is possible to love, hate and feel indifference towards an institution at the same time. It can be infuriating and exciting in equal measure. Being 'grateful' that we are here does not mean that we should view Cambridge uncritically, and criticism doesn't make us any less worthy of our places at university. The impetus behind student activism comes from a desire to make the institution better. So to anyone belonging to a marginalised group who is engaged in resistance work – sure people will roll their eyes, accuse you of whinging, make you feel like your well-founded complaints are an annoyance but remember Alice Walker when she wrote "no person is your friend that demands your silence."[48] You do not need the company of people who are unwilling to engage with the issues that are important to you.

However subtle or overt the calls are for you to be quiet, to keep your head down, to get your degree and then your law internship and wander off into the City, keep talking. Scream it from the rooftops, show your anger and your frustration openly because as a wise friend once told me, anger is the difference between people who say they want to change things and those who actually do. Use the platforms and magic legitimacy that Cambridge gives you to right wrongs, to point out the ridiculousness of this place because in doing so, you reclaim a little

[48] Walker, Alice. *In Search of Our Mothers' Gardens: Womanist Prose*, 2011.

piece of Cambridge for yourself. The more we criticise this institution the more it feels like ours. I can call Cambridge institutionally racist and still happily volunteer my time at open days.[49]

Women of colour and other oppressed groups: being at Cambridge does not have to "kill your spirit," as Fabian Romero reminds us.[50] I'm learning that you can be invested in social justice, endeavour to understand structural oppression and still love Eliot[51]. Become a saboteur who uses a variety of tactics; work within the bounds of the curriculum if you cannot work against it and subvert it when you can. You do not have to reconstruct yourself to fit an arbitrary Cambridge mould. Rebel with your language, your clothing, in anyway possible; show that there a thousand ways to be a Cambridge student because there are. It is okay to be angry. It is okay to be angry. It is okay to be angry. You can be angry and grateful at the same time.

---

[49] A day where prospective students can look around Cambridge colleges, departments and meet current students.

[50] A quote from a blog post by Queer Indigenous writer, performance artist and activist, Fabian Romero, https://fabianswriting.tumblr.com/

[51] Mary Anne Evans known by her pen name 'George Eliot' was a Victorian novelist, translator and poet.

The Legacy of Toni Morrison's 'Sugar-Brown Mobile Girls', or Teaching My Hair How to Curl Again

Odelia Younge

*These sugar-brown Mobile girls move through the streets without a stir…
They go to land-grant colleges, normal schools, and learn how to do the
white man's work with refinement…Here they learn the rest of the lesson
begun in those soft houses with porch swings and pots of bleeding heart: how
to behave. The careful development of thrift, patience, high morals, and good
manners. In short, how to get rid of the funkiness. The dreadful funkiness of
passion, the funkiness of nature, the funkiness of the wide range of
human emotions*

*Wherever it erupts, this Funk, they wipe it away; where it crusts, they
dissolve it; wherever it drips, flowers, or clings, they find it and fight it until
it dies. They fight this battle all the way to the grave. The laugh that is a
little too loud; the enunciation a little too round; the gesture little too gen-
erous. They hold their behind in for fear of a sway too free; when they wear
lipstick, they never cover the entire mouth for fear of lips too thick, and they
worry, worry, worry about the edges of their hair*[52]

–Toni Morrison

The first time I came into the personal awareness that my body would
become a symbol of sexualised property, I was around 14 and on
vacation in Florida with my family. I had left the hotel to collect an
order of pizza for everyone around the corner. As I made my way back
to the hotel, a car full of men leaned over and started yelling
obscenities at me, hurling phrases such as "Hey, want to fuck?" or
"How much for the whole car?" I froze. Never before had I been

---

[52] Morrison, Toni. *The Bluest Eye*. London: Pan Books, 1990. Print.

acutely aware of such a thing. I tried to become invisible. I stopped walking, hoping they would keep driving. They did keep driving as their red light turned green, but as they turned the corner they still yelled and laughed at me: "Last chance to give some head." As if even a first chance was some kind of honour. That was my first encounter of that type, and it would hardly be my last. Stand too long on a street corner waiting to cross, and I would have men try to solicit me for sex. I would dress up to go out with friends to spend the evening fending off unwanted advances.

In the summer after my sophomore year of undergraduate at Harvard, I travelled to Corsica to be an au pair. I was excited. I had only ever been to the United Kingdom, and here I was headed to a fancy island that others only got to view in photographs.

Things turned ugly fast though.

I got scared when I found myself on an isolated part of the island. The mother of the family I worked for became malicious and would tell me I had to take a sponge and clean around the edges of the entire house inside and out. She would make me take a toothbrush and do the same, despite being only hired to watch her children and tutor them in English. Her four sons were what some would refer to as 'curious' the female body, but what I would say was a product of their indoctrination into the patriarchy, where my body was rightfully theirs to explore. I would turn around to a naked young boy's penis pressed against me. I would endure them "falling" into my chest, their child and adolescent-sized hands grabbing at every part of my body, leaving invisible marks of shame. They would laugh with each other about it, glaring at me, daring me to make a scene or draw attention to the acts that transpired daily.

So I covered up. I convinced myself it was me, and if only I did not show so much skin (despite the fact I took them to the beach every day in 115 degrees Fahrenheit weather), things would be different. It was the feeling that I must cover up lest I draw attention to my body; the deeply-felt societal lessons of body shaming, evoking images of Toni Morrison's sugar-brown Mobile girls who dare not laugh or wear anything too tight for fear of sexualisation.[53] As a young black woman, I had inherited the belief that my sexuality was something to be ashamed of, and it made me doubt the deep, uncomfortable feelings I had each time a man advanced toward me or touched me without consent. How dare I confront someone for a consent society told both of us these men had?

Thinking back on this time now, most days I am fine. But there are days that I am back on beaches that have lost their beauty, where hands remind me that what is mine has been taken many times without consent.

It did not happen overnight, but eventually instead of quelling the Funk[54] that Morrison's sugar-brown Mobile girls were too afraid to embrace — the Funk that is our blackness — I instead embraced my body as a wonderful part of who I am, without it being the sole generator of who I am. A black woman's body tends to become that faster and deeper than other women's bodies. The oversexualisation of black girls and women is a centuries old tale, long before even the potent image of the Hottentot Venus.[55] Our young daughters are seen as women far before they should wear that label. This, despite the fact we are made by society to feel that there is something inherently undesirable about us. Yet the features we are told from birth are 'ugly' suddenly become desirable upon the skin colour and bodies of another. In moments when we come together to celebrate black womanhood, such moments of joy are met with opposition because *didn't they tell you that a black woman has nothing that she should celebrate?*

---

[53] 'Sugar brown mobile girls' is a reference to a passage in Toni Morrison's The Bluest Eye, that describes these women who are focused on 'behaving' and controlling and modifying their blackness to imitate white, dominant culture.

[54] The 'Funk' referred to here is a phrase from Toni Morrison's *The Bluest Eye* and describes emotion and truth.

[55] Sarah Baartman, stage-named the Hottentot Venus, was an African woman from the Khoikhoi tribe of South Africa's Eastern Cape. She was brought to Europe under false pretenses and paraded around in 'freak shows' due to fascination and obsession with her protuberant buttocks.

Because of the often jagged and long journey that stands between a black woman and embracing her self-worth, I became increasingly compelled to speak on these matters as someone who has and continues to go through these moments when I am reduced to an individual's desire to paint me as body, not as human. I am not responsible for the thoughts and actions of others based on my physical appearance. I am not, and never have been.

At Cambridge, I experienced oversexualisation from my peers. One person in particular, my floormate who was a white mathematician from Belgium, continuously did this to me. It started as comments whenever I saw him in the morning about what I was wearing. He liked to say that I clearly dressed for the men I wanted to draw attention from that day. When I tried to explain to him how I dressed for myself, and if I wore a short skirt it was because I loved my long legs, he said it was not possible. (Things are always impossible when your mindset is closed to other worlds besides your own.) His frequent comments on my clothing were also uncomfortable to me because they meant my presence to him was reduced to nothing more than my body. History has taught me to have a healthy fear of this. I would have avoided the kitchen, but I refused to be marginalised in my own home. But black women have often changed our daily practices and reduced our spaces of existence for the demands of others, and the safety of ourselves.

One particular moment that highlights the constant issue this posed occurred during Halloween. I was never allowed to dress up when I was a child, so I thought I would use the excuse as an adult to do some costuming. I decided to buy a costume with the girls who lived upstairs, and we were all going to be burlesque dancers in leopard-print clothing. The costume consisted of a corset, a tutu, a tail and a bowtie. The corset, being a corset, did its job to enhance the fact that I have breasts, and breasts that are larger than normal for a woman of my size. I spent that night with people staring at my breasts, making comments about them (at my birthday party the next month, a friend would even make a speech almost solely dedicated to my breasts in costume), and one man told me a week later that he had saved a photo of me in the costume on his phone. At another Halloween party, my friend and I went as zombie mermaids, and our outfits included raggedly cut tops that exposed our stomachs, and seashells and crazy paint. As I was having a friend rip the shirt in the kitchen, the same Belgian floormate looked at me with disgust on his face and asked, "Why do you even bother to wear clothes?" (Later in the year, he would go on to tell me that I mentioned being a black woman too much and he believed the obstacles I mentioned existed in my imagination and were not rooted in reality.)

For many at Cambridge, I was this overly sexual being, though to me, I was dressing to flatter how I wanted my body to look. And if I was not interested in sleeping with the men who mainly perpetuated these ideas, I was a lesbian. I wore a crop top (I love crop tops) to a party and a female floormate warned me that the men would talk about it. When I talked to some men at the college, I could tell that I made them uncomfortable because I dared to embrace and feel comfortable with my sexuality. Something society had told them *they* should own. That is always the paradox. I am the one in these situations with the legitimate threat of something happening to them in a world consumed by rape culture, yet I get branded the perpetrator of the crime I can only name as *being*.

I am comfortable in my own skin. I love my body. And I want that love to translate into future generations so that black girls can be children and know that play and imagination do not have to result in death. And this love of my body must also come with the ability to love without fear of loss that which springs forth from my body. The State has historically existed to allow the ownership of black women's bodies, to stand by as those bodies have children ripped from them at childbirth — forced to be a vessel for the enjoyment of others, while we cried then and cry now for our taken children. Social justice and reproductive rights are profoundly linked for black women. We know we must assert our right to say this is my body, and I alone control it.

It is an ongoing battle, however, for that recognition from the personal to the public. Such an ongoing battle that I no longer take part in the war — at least not in the way society has historically wanted me to. We are told to treat our bodies like temples, draped in modesty, but I instead am moved by the words of Beau Taplin who wrote, "Listen to me, your body is not a temple. Temples can be destroyed and desecrated. Your body is a forest—thick canopies of maple trees and sweet scented wildflowers sprouting in the underwood. You will grow back, over and over, no matter how badly you are devastated." [56]

When I meet men, especially white men, it is often the same, tired story of their fascination—their fetish—with black women. *I had a black girlfriend once. You're so sassy. My friend likes exotic women.* The list goes on. They do not wish to remember the hands of their ancestors on the necks of my foremothers. The unwanted touch and non-consensual penetration. There were no black mistresses despite how they write about us. Only black women staring into darkness, lying on their backs while the weight of death was upon them.

And yet, in many ways, white men echo that spirit of desired dominance, born from the allowance of the patriarchy to take as they please and masculinity that tells them that I somehow want it. It is hard to reconcile the two to date them. There was a Twitter post some of us FLY girls loved that said, "Yeah he's cute, but is he an intersectional feminist who understands white privilege & strongly dislikes the patriarchy?" Simply speaking, if the answer is no, we keep moving.

In spite of the markers of history, I have dated a few white men. There was one who in the middle of an argument told me to 'stop being such a black girl.' I dated another who whenever I brought up racism said he really liked me but did not want to deal with "this" for the whole relationship. I can only assume the "this" he was referring to was the reality of my life. It is nearly impossible to reconcile that there is a power dynamic in what happens to blackness in white spaces. Impossible to pretend that these attractions are not rooted in years

---

[56] Beau Taplin via www.beautaplin.com

of oppression and erasure of our own beauty. I have found that it is important for me to date those who truly appreciate Odelia, the individual black woman, who loves and navigates her life with a sense that blackness is enough.[57]

Black women are seldom found in spaces such as Cambridge, and once here attract the same type of attention we draw in other spaces. Academia does not change such things. We are still *black girl dangerous*. Yes, it is important for my body to take up space as a reminder that this body belongs to me and me alone. The 'sugar-brown Mobile girls' reject those parts of them that others attach to blackness, but it is their blackness that would allow them to feel the full magnitude of their being: the curly edges of their hair, the rhythmic sway of their body, the fullness in their bold lips, and so much more. To be one with that physical prowess is an integral part of liberation. It is in the history of the curly edges of my own hair that I embraced an integral part of my journey.

******

Photos of toddler me show her with ringlet curls and colourful ribbons and plastic clips. Hair shiny from your standard black hair products. Edges laid flat against the sides of my hair. Creamy crack[58] with that strong smell. Mix it in and lather it onto my hair.

It burns. It burns. It burns.

And with each burn it scorches my hair flat. It strips away my hair follicles ability to curl into itself and around my head. It says no lye, but there is the lie that one could somehow chemically reduce their hair to acceptance, when instead all that was left was the smell of something burnt, like houses burning across the Atlantic hundreds of years ago. Looking like white people more with stick straight hair, shaking around one's face if one had that "good" press on that "good" hair. If the edges started to turn back (they always ruined the façade

---

[57] Thank you for being the first place I read these words, Hari Ziyad.
[58] 'Creamy crack' here refers to relaxer products that chemically straighten hair.

first), you could easily "touch that up" or hot iron it back down into its place; the uprising stopped in its tracks.

Sometimes I see online forums where black women blame their mothers for putting that first relaxer on their hair. But we are our mothers' daughters, even when we move away from their practices. In fact, when they gave us the sparks for the fires they could not light themselves, that Alice Walker wrote about, they did so in order for us to continue in the fight for our own liberation.[59] I have no resentment towards my mother for relaxing my hair for so many years. In fact, there were many years I would beg her to put the relaxer in my hair at a faster pace, and she would tell me no. My mother, like all of us, had been indoctrinated into European beauty standards. Straight hair is best. If you must have curls, they must be acceptable curls, meaning fine, without frizz, and 'behaved.' It meant a straight nose and light skin. But the cheapest of these to get was straight hair. I envied the few black women I could find in magazines with their hair laid perfectly, swinging from side to side. I envied my mom for her naturally straight hair. Why could I not be like her?

By the time I was in college, I had started to relax my hair less. I had started to notice how stringy my hair would feel after the relaxer treatments, and how it felt stunted in its growth. I could feel the damage of years of heat processing. This practice turned to almost never in college since I had lost the help of my mother and getting my hair relaxed was expensive. I turned instead to the practice of the Dominican blowout, becoming an expert at locating the best priced salons, not caring how long it took me to get my hair done each visit or how hot their hair tools got. The more smoke, the better the hair 'hang.'

When I moved to Ghana after graduation, I was praised for how much hair I had, as it had become healthier since letting go of the relaxer. But I hated that I was being praised for how *straight* my hair was, its prize and worth being in its complete absence of curls or

___
[59] Alice Walker, *'In Search of Our Mothers' Gardens: The Creativity of Black Women in the South*: 1974

kinks. I started paying attention more to images of black women who had embraced their natural hair, but I didn't think I could do it. When I moved to Miami to teach, my assistant principal was a formidable black woman whose presence was always felt when she entered a room. This queen proudly wore her hair in its natural form, and it was not the curls that were often praised as acceptable, but the kinks and curls that grew as they pleased, relinquished from any prisons of creamy crack and lye. She would tell me how I should just cut all my hair off and start over; go back to the beginning. I didn't know what the beginning was. I would repeatedly respond that her hair was amazing, but that it would not look right on me. Looking back now, I can clearly hear myself saying, in this way, that my own natural hair was somehow an abomination of nature that I could not accept.

As my consciousness grew I began to feel that for me, my hair was the last frontier. The summer before I left for Cambridge I decided to do two smaller chops instead of one big chop to ease myself into this new journey. After my second chop, the hairdresser said once my hair grew, it would not grow with any more relaxer in it. I sat in the hairdresser's chair for a while, staring into the mirror at my reflection and then looking down at the chunks of hair that held such history. They felt like they belonged to someone else. I was excited for the new hairs to relearn who they were at the beginning.

I knew that Cambridge would be a desert of help for black women and our hair, so I covered my hair up to give it time to grow out more. I was fascinated by the amount of people who actually believed I had straight hair (Clearly a symptom of not knowing people who are not like them, or ignoring the existence of those who were. You do not get to claim ignorance at that stage of your life when you have such privileges.). In the spring, I was ready to let my hair breathe, having more time while working on my dissertation to learn to take care of my natural hair. I had the largest smile on my face when I saw the tiny tendrils of hair. I knew this was just the freshness and that it would take some time for my hairs to remember how they truly grew. And I was prepared for people's reactions. People who exclaimed about my hair in not so complimentary ways, or ones who said they liked my straight hair better (which has its own indications). But I was in love, and nothing could stop that feeling of love. Not even when I had an argument with my mother who did not like my hair and urged me to go to the hairdresser. I cried for what felt like an entire day after that, feeling as though this journey would be a constant battle with someone whose opinion really mattered. But I prayed and I knew, like myself, that what she needed was time.

Learning how to take care of my hair has been a long journey, and one that was not helped by the fact I found only one place in Cambridge to buy products for my hair. It was not helped by the fact I was constantly teaching people things about my hair, stopping people from touching my hair without permission, and being the resident black expert. I had learned so much about their standard of beauty that it had taken over my younger life. It is a shame that knowledge that went the other way was almost never personally sought by my white peers. What I had intended to be a personal journey of learning to love the hair I was blessed with that I think is amazing and so versatile, became a public spectacle.

With everything developed by or belonging to black women, there are many who try to take away the power in wearing our natural hair. There are those who wish to make the community divisive. But I am here for all my sisters — bald-headed to Brazilian weave and everything in between. When it comes to black women's bodies and anything that extends from that, however, everyone else has to have a say. The divisive ones say natural hair is only about another set of individuals making money or a new look and way of discriminating within the group. With anything, though, there are ideas that do create controversy and divides — the attention to length and 'appropriate' natural hairstyles, to name a few — but that is for us as black women to navigate.

Black women's hair has always been political. Therefore, any rejection of the dominant European beauty norms — which can take the form of our natural hair — is an act of political resistance, whether it is labelled so or not. There is no power in the apolitical when it comes to our hair. While wearing our natural hair may not always be a movement, it is a state of being. Of loving and embracing what we have been given. It is our heritage, and a collective memory that has been buried and burned for too long. We must reclaim it, celebrate it, shout it, like others who came before us, and especially when it is a spectacle.

Sisters: Do not pull in your behind. Do not under-paint with lipstick the luscious lines of your thick lips. When they say that you are some type of vixen, an emasculator of man, or unsuitable for decent company, laugh as loud and as carefree as you wish.

PART FOUR:
Creating and Speaking Our Own

each tide broke your will
and your back — it is
easy to drown in silence.

-

languish in language –
hope not to break ground but to
remain here, grounded.

-Jun Pang

Space

Bright white fantasy distorts, creates the necessity to speak where there isn't
one. Mouth ajar, eyebrows furrowed. He doesn't even know the weight of his
arms and legs. It's anticipated now, the interruption. [Deep breath]
-

I look at them as they sit some shy unable to speak for fear they might choke
tentative and then wide eyed/brash/nervous/swallowing hard, biting
        down harder.
then, she flings her words across the room so fast she can't be interrupted.
teeth flailing. I want to ask, what skin did you shed just then?
Share a piece of what made you untouchable.

Lola Olufemi

On the Need for Safe Spaces after Crossing Borders
Waithera Sebatindira

The concept of a safe space can be a difficult one to explain and, as a result, a number of negative connotations are often wrongly attached to them. Simply put, the term "safe space" denotes an area or forum open only to members of a particular marginalised group where they can speak and act freely without fear of being attacked, questioned, or made to feel unwelcome or ignored (as they may be made to feel outside of a safe space). It also denotes a space where members of that group can draw strength from each other and, if so inclined, put together plans for resistance.

That being said, there's a general view that safe spaces are a form of self-imposed segregation. When the road to equality is ostensibly paved through integration, it may appear counter-productive for groups of minorities to deliberately separate themselves from the majority. Another criticism levelled against safe spaces is that they are "echo chambers". That is, places where people rebound the same ideas off of each other, knowing that they will be met with agreement; no new thoughts emerge and things remain the same. A more well-meaning complaint may come from allies who resent being excluded from spaces despite their commitment to help that group in their cause. At first blush, these criticisms do seem valid, but in reality they evince a lack of understanding as to the purpose and effect of safe spaces. It is, however, an ignorance that can be easily displaced.

FLY was one safe space in particular that defied all of these. Although the reasons for its birth are, at face value, apolitical, FLY is revolutionary for a number of reasons. A group of women of colour (WoC) unapologetically occupying space in a university originally built exclusively for white men is radical, as is voicing our thoughts on our experiences and having them validated where they would otherwise be dismissed or misunderstood. That being said, FLY attracts a range of women from incredibly varied backgrounds. Some identify with The Struggle[60] while others feel they've been sheltered from it. In meetings, it was usually the case that everyone's politics were generally in alignment, but as the group has grown, opinions have become more diverse.

One of my favourite things about FLY is the way that it validates personal emotions that one might have had but never fully understood. Outside of spaces like FLY it's difficult to find the requisite language to describe our experiences, not only in ways that allow non-WoC to understand them, but more importantly that allow us to break those experiences down for ourselves. You come to FLY and someone will put into words a feeling you've had for years, and introduce you to other people who will explain the myriad ways in which your existence in a space like Cambridge can be radical. For me, FLY was a place of learning. Consequently, if it is an "echo chamber", it is one to the extent to which any place of learning is such a "chamber"; the repetition of facts and experiences is never gratuitous. Each time a story was shared, someone in the group was growing in their political consciousness and, consequently, in their knowledge of themselves.

More than this, in an effort to combat the ignorance prevalent at Cambridge, which is at the root of most of our more negative experiences, FLY continues to increase its presence at the university and make public some of the ideas discussed at meetings and on the Facebook group. The Fly. Blog[61] — which accepts contributions only from WoC but allows people of all genders and races to engage with

[60] A colloquial term used to describe the (often classed) pressures of racism faced by black people.

its content — elevates the concerns of WoC and introduces the rest of the student body to our unique experiences. From its first day online it's been highly popular and continues to grow. At the end of my time as facilitator for FLY, there was talk of beginning to receive contributions from WoC on a national level and introduce the blog to a wider audience. We are seeing its international reach expand. All of this shows that the messages FLY girls are sharing resonate with WoC far beyond the borders of this university town.

WoC in particular need to organise because our voices are so often erased in wider liberation movements. Mainstream feminism fails to include WoC, instead centring the experiences of white (middle-class) women as if those experiences were universal. Campaigns for racial equality also exclude WoC. These campaigns focus almost exclusively on men of colour, showing that they're permeated with patriarchal norms that value the lives of men above those of women. Thus, in choosing to tend to our own needs when they are not being met by others, we are not segregating ourselves. Rather, we are showing how much we value our wellbeing and our liberation. These experiences of erasure mean that FLY aims to be inclusive in every way: the space belongs to all WoC, including those who exist at other intersections concerning (for example) class, sexuality, and/or gender identity. In my eyes, FLY's greatest strength has always drawn from the diversity of its members.

With regard to allies, while their support is genuinely appreciated, their presence within a safe space can be counter-productive, particularly for women who seek out safe spaces not for political reasons but simply to find solidarity with women with similar backgrounds to their own. Even the best ally won't share the lived experiences of a WoC and safe spaces cease to be safe once you continuously have to explain your experiences and justify your emotional reactions to others.

The Problem with Debate
Lola Olufemi

The academy is built on the idea that debate is crucial to the acquisition of knowledge. Much of Cambridge is structured around this. In our essays, we're asked how far can you take one idea and stretch it? We're confronted in supervisions: 'How strong is the argument you form after reading primary and secondary material and can you defend it?' In the context of the way we learn, everything is debatable. The idea that withdrawal from debate represents surrender haunts us. But what we see as fodder for debate is influenced, crucially, by power. If you feel like you can debate every single topic calmly and rationally without stress or anxiety, well done. You're one of the lucky ones.[62]

When we think about what it means to platform certain voices, we can draw obvious links between what is said and what is done. Our speech acts have consequences, they do not simply disappear into the ether when uttered. This is why we have a developed a system to categorise types of speech. 'Hate speech' is widely recognised as harmful and this comes from an understanding that words matter. What is up for debate for one person may be off limits for another, not because one values intellectual rigour more than the other, but because the parameters of the debate are inextricably linked to the threat of harm - physical and emotional. For example, as a black woman, debating whether or racism still exists in the twenty-first century is dangerous

---

[62] In *Black Feminist Thought*, Patricia Hill Collins argues that valuing objectivity and provable arguments benefits white men the most. She posits an alternative means of understanding knowledge that she refers to as 'black feminist thought,' which centers the lived experiences of marginalised people and treats them as valuable truths.

because it assumes that there will be no material consequences to this discussion. It assumes that black people are no longer at risk of being subjected to violence by the racists who will be emboldened by such a discussion. That is not my reality. From police brutality, racist economic and housing policies, exploitation, colonial legacies and cultural domination, oppression is a tangible phenomena; we do not need to fan its flames. We need to extinguish it.

When we debate something, we assume that all speakers enter the discussion on equal footing. Race, gender and a host of other conditions influence what we say, how we say it and whose speech is viewed as legitimate and accepted without criticism. In a letter to Mary Daly in 1979, Audre Lorde theorised the concept of 'emotional cost' to black women who entered debates with white feminists about their inattentiveness to race when theorising about gender. She concluded that when one enters into the debate to defend the truth of their reality, be it race, gender or sexuality, the consequences of that debate are far worse for them. It is not only physically and emotionally taxing, it affirms the myth that there is a neutral terrain where such things may be explored when no such terrain exists.

Structures organise our lives, we cannot escape them. It seems odd to argue about whether race and gender still affect our lives when every single day some of us deal with the repercussions of what it means to be a person of colour or a woman or both. What we defend is important. It is easy to debate abstract ideas because we cannot grasp them; this means we can poke at them, twist them around, play devil's advocate, imagine a number of situations in which X-Y-Z could occur and how this might change the argument and so on. But race and gender are not simply ideas, though they have been constructed, they are constructions with life or death consequences.

It is important to recognise that we live in a hierarchical society where all kinds of discourse – social, political, and economic – strengthen the voices of some whilst erasing others. How then, can we ever conceive of debate on equal terms? Maybe it's scary to admit that debate is not everything. Winning an argument in the bar with your friend is only a victory on a microscopic level. Often it comes down to one's ability to frame an argument, rather than the truth of experiences. There is an alarming trend where institutions, clubs, societies and even academic journals are asking "controversial" figures to speak in the name of 'balanced' debate. This leads to an environment where well known publications feel able to post articles that pose questions like "was slavery good for the economy?" [63] When we dignify such questions with a response, we ignore the pain of seeing your being and the violence you experience held up as fodder for "rigorous intellectual debate." What is wit and style to one person undermines the existence of another. This reliance on an enlightenment-style rationality does not take into account that when we ask these reductive questions, we suggest that is possible to pose them without ideological repercussions.

Activists on the left have used deplatforming as a tool against fascists and perpetrators of hate speech because they understand what is at stake when their views are legitimised by the media and liberals who demand a 'balance.' When you come from a background that has told you that winning the debate is the only measure of success, it becomes difficult to think of other methods of acquiring knowledge as valuable. Listening, for example. Because the act of listening is feminised, it is synonymous with passivity but listening provides the key to recentering the lives of those most at risk in our society instead of those who put them at risk. Empathy is more radical than intellectual rigour. Remember that often, refusing to engage in debate is not a sign of intellectual weakness, but an act of survival.

There are probably a number of other criticisms that people might try and throw at a space like FLY, but, ultimately, a forum that supports and empowers WoC, that allows us to recharge and be understood, can only be a good thing.

---

[63] https://www.economist·com/free-exchange/2013/09/27/did-slavery-make-economic-sense

Describe Your Anger in Less than 500 Words. Use 'Point, Evidence, Explanation'

Suhaiymah Manzoor-Khan

For me FLY was more than just a network of women of colour, more than even solidarity and empathy – it was new life. A learning process, yes, but also a creating process. FLY was a space, a group of people and a feeling. It was where I was reminded of me. Reminded it was okay to be angry, reminded there was reason to be angry, that it was okay to hurt and that my hurt was real.

I remember when I came back from my first FLY meeting. My heart was genuinely thumping in my chest. I was smiling more widely than I had for some time and I felt as if someone had offered me a new life-line. As if I was back at that day when I had received my Cambridge offer and had hope that it could be what I dreamt it could be. It felt as if someone was whispering to me, saying I had been right all along. I had not been alone. I tried to explain it to my college friends, tried to convey my euphoria, but I suppose this was the first of many times that I realised what was so special about FLY was that you had to be in it to understand it.

Although FLY was a network for women and non-binary people of colour and vaguely feminist in that sense, the first thing FLY taught me was not about black feminism or radical politics, it was the value of my own experiences. When I first started going to those tea-shop meetings of four or five girls huddled around a table, I had never heard of bell hooks, Audre Lorde or Patricia Hill Collins, [64] and I had no idea what an 'intersection' was outside of the context of traffic. The first lessons I learned from FLY were solely about the legitimacy of my reality. I had grown so used to being shushed and making myself nod along when people told me 'it won't have been to do with race', that by my second year I had reached the stage where I silenced myself. I policed my own experiences by defending the actions of others against my gut feelings and defending the nature of the university against my emotions.

Coming from that headspace then, FLY was liberation. There, the nods of other women, their stories which echoed my own, and my belief in their experiences, taught me I had been right all along. It taught me that even when the whole world tried to convince me 'it wasn't to do with race', 'no, it didn't seem awkward', 'no, they didn't look at you differently' or 'you're being too sensitive', my instinct was right.

FLY not only acknowledged this reality that I had been institution-ally manipulated to ignore, it also gave me words to articulate those experiences too. For instance, I learnt the term 'microaggression'. 'Microaggressions' explained those interactions which racially profiled, stereotyped, patronised, excluded, othered, dehumanised and tokenised me in different ways. At last I had a word to describe daily experiences myself and other racialised people know well. Experiences that come with a familiar feeling of noticing yourself being treated differently to others. Of noticing a loaded phrase, an impolite interaction which is more than that, being spoken over, not listened to, having your idea credited to someone else, being spoken down to, asked dehumanising questions – the list goes on. White people may call it sensitivity; white people may call it playing the race card. The white people I know and love called it neither of these things, but in calling it nothing they were

---

[64] bell hooks, *Feminist Theory: From Margin to Center*, 2000; Audre Lorde, *Sister Outsider*, 1984; Patricia Hill Collins, *Black Feminist Thought: Knowledge, Consciousness, and the Politics of Empowerment*, 2000.

unable to see, feel or support me in the way FLY could. Words have power.

In hearing the words and voices of other FLY girls, I learnt to raise my own. Uniquely, in this space, unlike other spaces in Cambridge, raising one's own voice provided a step up for others rather than drowning them out. Our voices fortified each other. The consequence of such validation and understanding was that in the autumn of 2014 I found a year's worth of beliefs about myself and Cambridge come crashing down. I recognised how much I had internalised the idea that I was not worthy of Cambridge, and that my being here was a benevolent favour. I now rejected that. I was worthy and the institution was oppressive.

'Pretend to write like one of those Eton-toffs you probably don't approve of', was an offhand suggestion from one of my supervisors when I asked what it was I could do to raise my essays from 2:1s to 1sts in my second year. The suggestion that I should unlearn everything about myself, that I should detach my life, my understanding and my view of the world from myself to do well at Cambridge told me everything I needed to know about the university's institutional biases. It told me that this wasn't a place opening up to people like me. Even if there were surface changes, or more different people in the university, it was built on and relied upon a system naturalised to benefit a certain type of person. A place that would reward you based on who you were, not the myth of meritocracy it suggested. It was therefore a place erasing the existence of those that made it uncomfortable – placing the onus to be different upon them (us) and not itself. Subsequently, it was a place staunchly perpetuating an elitist hierarchy of legitimacy that placed privately-educated white men's opinions, beliefs and knowledge of the world at the very top.

In short, what I was being taught was that the 'best' or most 'valuable' way of writing was a way that depended on the confidence of eighteen years or more of socialisation into a world which at every level and through every institution tells you that you are valuable, important, clever, special and deserving. A world that I had not and would never witness.

Had I been told to 'write like an Etonian man' a year previously, I may have swallowed it and tried to change myself. But FLY gave me the confidence to hear what that really meant and the broader pattern it reflected. It gave me the belief in myself to see how such a comment displaced the broader issue of bias by placing the responsibility for rectifying institutional disadvantage on the individual: me. But I rejected that. I wasn't here to slip through the net and 'fit in', but to be true to myself whatever that entailed. That meant recognising that the vision being laid out for me in that comment and in the institution more generally was the valorisation of a form of being, writing, arguing and debating that was dependent on a position in the world which benefited from centuries of racism, socio-economic injustice, and patriarchy.

In daily Cambridge reality the most tangible way this translated into practice was the valorisation of a form of argumentation and debate (in academic writing, in conversation, in The Cambridge Union) that was best suited to those whose privilege distanced them from most of the things they discussed. It was a form of debate which prioritised being right and winning, rather than the nuances of truth. It prioritised convincing and impressing one's audience rather than creating a dialogue and thus meant reduction, oversimplification, selective truth-telling, and arrogance. Such factors are best used by those with no investment in the topic they're discussing. Therefore the debating I was being taught to emulate and value was both grotesquely simple but also unnervingly powerful. It was a form which turned experiences into buzzwords which could be abstracted from their contexts to be bandied around by tailcoats and bowties over champagne and canapes. The sort of debating you see in parliament.

Just before the General Election of 2015 I remember getting em- broiled in a discussion about the impact of austerity. At one point I consciously realised that the discussion could go nowhere because

I was here to negotiate and reach understanding, whilst the person I was talking to was intent on 'winning' the point. This meant that to them the whole debate was abstract. It wasn't about real experiences and people - they couldn't be convinced of that. Instead, it was about 'proving a point' and getting the First.[65]

In fact, I remember vividly giving up and saying 'food banks are real, they're not abstract concepts you can debate about, they exist and people use them'. That the conversation ever reached that level of detachment and privilege where we could be 'debating' about whether and how bad it was that food banks were being used, demonstrated the problem. It proved the danger of the glorification of neat, persuasive arguments where the only facts counted are quantitative, statistical, and previously acknowledged as 'truths' by those in power, rather than truths that are qualitative, nuanced, or not known to us because they are experiences not our own.

Indeed, this glorification of selective-evidence-based, point-by-point, persuasion-heavy argumentation at Cambridge meant that even those discussions about personal experience were forced into the framework of 'academic exercises'. Consequently, the lived experience of those of us whose lives were marginalised from the mainstream and deemed invalid due to institutional bias, selective histories, and privilege, were completely devalued. The argumentation valued at Cambridge saw many of our experiences as women of colour trampled on by those who told us they were not persuasive enough, merely anecdotal, too personal and emotional. Our expertise in our own lives was mocked and our knowledges and epistemologies[66] viewed as invalid. Thus, for many FLY girls the trauma of having the sorts of conversations we had in FLY meetings, outside of FLY, was the trauma of having our experiences put up for debate – our very humanity erased in the process.

---

[65] Known as a "first", a first class is the highest honours degree achievable.
[66] Epistemologies refers to theories of knowledge - the way we 'know' things, what counts as 'knowing' and 'knowledge'.

I remember, for example, coming back from a trip to Sainsburys one day and relating an experience of Islamophobia to a friend. A man on the street had harassed me aggressively demanding "why does your Allah tell you to kill people?". My telling of this story was not deemed "proof" enough of Islamophobia. My friend was not convinced this was Islamophobia despite it being the reproduction of a racist stereotype, racial profiling, an accusation made based on my identity and nothing more, and the fact it wasn't really a question but an attempt to intimidate. But because it was 'anecdotal' and based on my feeling and instinctual knowledge — my friend presumed to debate it with me. Not just questioning and analysing the situation which I wouldn't have had a problem with per se and could have been fruitful or illuminating - but treating it in a way that undermined and invalidated my lived experience, leaving me not only shaken up by the encounter, but additionally alienated and alone.

When we invalidate the importance and 'truth' of feelings and anecdotes, we reinforce the erasure and are complicit in the silencing of oppressed people. This is because feelings are ways of knowing. Anxiety and stress are ways our bodies tell us we have experienced traumatic incidents. Feelings of pain are how we know we are hurt. Feelings are how we know we love, or care, or need to change our circumstances, or act, or intervene. Yet when it comes to questions of oppression, discrimination and marginalisation, feelings are deemed the antithesis to 'logic'.

Marginalised people are especially silenced through this perception because our histories have been systematically excluded from what counts as History. Our epistemologies have been physically and psychologically erased (e.g. through destruction, or theft and reattribution of manuscripts, archives, libraries, lives, languages and artifacts; as well as institutional exclusion of colonised people's histories, legends, poetry, art, linguistics, bodies of medicinal knowledge, ways of documenting social change etc). This erasure is complex because there is no documentation of the process itself.

For example, no histories recount how histories themselves are written, or what choices go into deciding which materials deserve archiving and which do not. In this sense, there are many ways in which we do not even know what we do not know of colonised and enslaved people's pasts. This is the outcome of colonialism being embedded in our academic institutions - but everyday actions also perpetuate this silencing by simply upholding power relations of domination, erasure, and hierarchies of 'truth'.

In my time at Cambridge, I saw testimonial accounts of mental health issues consistently dismissed as 'anecdotal'. This meant there was no accountability for the high rates of depression experienced by students - exemplifying how hierarchisation of certain forms of evidence are not just accidental, but have political functions: in this case the function of displacing responsibility for improving the wellbeing of students.

I also encountered the same feeling as many people of colour regarding lodging complaints about racism experienced at the hands of porters, supervisors, tutors or lecturers: what complaint could we make that would be seen as backed by strong enough "evidence"? We were used to our experiences been invalidated as anecdotal. We didn't have the benefit of being 'Eton-toffs' whose very opinions have the value that even our actual experiences didn't. This is how oppression upholds itself, and Cambridge is complicit because of its role in teaching future elites that the only ways of knowing and the only Truth is the truth that maintains the hierarchy of power which privileges them.

Subsequently, for me, meeting and sharing my truths with other women of colour at FLY was how I realised I was not alone, and how I realised my truths were true even in a context which condemned them as false (gaslighting[67] was another word I later learnt through FLY girls which articulated this form of institutional manipulation that

---

[67] A form of psychological manipulation that sows doubt in the targeted individual or members of a targeted group, making them question their own memory, perception of reality, and sanity.

that denied the authenticity of our realities). In hearing others and being heard, I realised that there was a story that we all had to tell and that the walls of this place were trying to shut us out on all sides. I also began to realise something else: the reason I had ignored and silenced this knowledge within myself for so long often came down to 'politeness'.

'Politeness' meant not getting angry publicly. It meant being dispassionate, detached and arguing calmly. This sort of 'politeness' is an important element of debating in the Cambridge-glorified way. Debating skills rely heavily on how an argument is presented – the less emotional-investment, the more 'logical' and thus, convincing.

Well, here was another point of conflict for me. Lived experience is never 'objective'. In fact, no opinion is ever built from a place free of positionality and thus a subjective view of the world. But since many at Cambridge really believed objectivity existed, if someone were to have an emotional investment in the conversation topic, if what they were talking about mattered to them and they longed to be understood rather than to 'convince', remaining politely dispassionate was both difficult and pointless. On the morning after the 2015 announcement of a Tory government I posted an angry status on Facebook deploring those who relished five more years of austerity and violent border controls. Whilst a majority of my friends approved the sentiment, there were many who did not. However, these people did not just refute, disagree, or engage with me. They expressly told me not to be angry. They told me this was not the place for anger and that my anger was proof of irrationality and unreasonableness. Instead of anger I should accept the fact of the matter and move on.

To be frank, I was shocked. I hadn't realised up until that point how sorely and obviously there was a fear of anger. How anger was threatening because it was the exposure of injustice – it was consequential. The reactions I received reeked of privilege and the fear of being made to consider, even for a moment, that privilege itself. They rejected the place of anger, because they refused to understand.

One girl even commented that elections were similar to football matches and we should remain just as dispassionate when one side 'won', or 'lost'. Her comment perfectly encapsulated the 'objectivity' that privilege makes possible.

Silencing doesn't have to be violent or overtly threatening. Disabling the dissent of the marginalised and oppressed often manifests through jokes or denial of anger which delegitimise it. Not only did these college peers dislike my anger, they attempted to invalidate it. Invalidating anger prioritises a way of thinking that is devoid of feeling, that glorifies an ability to detach oneself from the subject - due to a material reality in which such detachment is possible (in this case because of wealth/race/citizenship status). It is for these reasons that detachment and dispassion come hand in hand with 'debating persuasively'. It is for these reasons that it is urged by the educators of the elite — because doing so maintains the status quo.

Those shoving fingers to my lips argued with me exactly as I should have expected them to in Cambridge: abstractly and detached from the matter at hand. Those who urged me not to be angry benefitted from my passivity. Those who told me to respect their opinions benefitted from the subordination of mine.

For too long I did not call people out for fear of seeming rude. For too long I believed that keeping calm would give me more chance of being heard. But these decisions only benefited the oppressive status quo. Anger was only 'impolite' to them as code for 'threatening'. But to me anger was creative. A life-force. Anger was key to survival in an oppressive world. When I realised this; when I realised that I was angry and had reason to be; when I saw how hollow the modes of knowledge valued by Cambridge were and how detached we were taught to be – that was when I could understand it all. Cambridge was inherently and institutionally racist. Surface changes would not change this larger historical and epistemological truth.

For me, this realisation freed me from believing Cambridge was all that it claimed to be. Learning to fully believe my feelings and myself rather than what was deemed The Truth – an arrogant attempt at Godliness - was when I began to truly be alive at Cambridge. FLY was what resuscitated me.

PART FIVE:
Becoming Individuals within the Collective

they invented the east and the sun
to salvage their pallid earth; eyes

too narrow to see, the first people
to speak for mine.

-

for beauty —
we have frightened away too many wounds.

-

scuttling, with
no sense of pause

they are frantic.
to see the difference

is too much;
to breathe is to

be weak, and
naïve besides —

they smash ants
with hammers.

-*Jun Pang*

Collective Responsibility and Collective Pain
Odelia Younge

"And what shall we do, we who did not die? What shall we do now? How shall we grieve, and cry out loud, and face down despair? Is there an honorable, non-violent means towards mourning and remembering who and what we loved?"[68]

–June Jordan

I woke up to a missed call the morning after a day spent on an airplane coming back to America to see my first college roommate get married during the spring of my time at Cambridge. Before I left for my graduate studies I had spent a couple years in Miami as a Reading teacher. Education had always been part of my life path: I taught my first class, Introduction to Jazz History, when I was in high school, and I spent my years in undergraduate and the years following focused on transforming the education system in the U.S. and advocating for children's rights. Teaching in Miami constantly revealed to me the realities of black neighborhoods: struggling under crippling systemic oppression while also rich in tradition and culture and community. The school I taught in was no different. The principal would often note how people scoffed when they asked if anything good could come out of their town, but the students proved the question obsolete each year. There was so much good in that community.

The missed call was from an old colleague Dani who left the message, "Call me when you see this." I knew immediately that it would not be

---

[68] Jordan, June. *"Some of us did not die: New and selected essays."* (2003).

good. When you have worked where I have worked, you know that if it is from an old colleague, it must involve one of your old students, and that it will not be good.

My heart began racing and my fingers felt clammy as I picked up my phone to dial Dani's number.

"Hi, I got your message. What's going on?" I said, trying to make my voice come out in a steady, unshaking tone.

Dani didn't waste time, because we don't do that. Not in a world where things change in a matter of seconds — realities destroyed by the presence of daily situations.

Dead.

I had been so far removed with end of term papers and field research that I had not even heard the news that she had been a victim of a hit and run. The physical distance between Miami and Cambridge did not help. I had not lived the uncertainties of the last days of her life. I did not know the days that were filled with her face on the news while her mother begged for anyone with information to come forward. I did not spend the following days haunted by images of her bruised face laying on a hospital bed. In my mind, she went from the quiet girl with the quick smile and small handwriting, whose desk was right next to mine during fifth period, to dead — a reality destroyed in a matter of seconds. We had our rocky times, but we had come far in a year. There was so much we were both proud of.

The rest of the day I went about working on things that needed to get done in rote fashion. I remember telling my mom over the phone, and a few close friends over a message. That night was the first social event for my friend's wedding. Before the event, I went to dinner with my close friend James, who was hosting me at his house. It was like any typical time we have together, with laughter and smiles in abundance. I can't remember how, but the conversation switched to a more serious tone as I began telling him in long, winding sentences about the re-flooding of guilt that was washing over me for leaving my students. As I was talking, my chest began to tighten in all too familiar ways, and I looked down at my phone and my eyes fixed on a text from another close teaching friend. It was a link to one of the articles written about my student's death, followed by the question, "Did you have her?"

In that moment, I finally let the waves fully crash over me and I began crying in the middle of the restaurant, gulping air as tears fell in ragged bursts. James silently led me out of the restaurant into the cold night air as eyes turned to gaze upon me. In this moment, I had the privilege, the luxury, to come undone. I knew I would not have been afforded this moment under the questioning and hurting gaze of students had I still been teaching. We are never awarded such luxuries in the face of a system that tells us to "move on."

"I can't go. I can't do it. I can't smile and chat when I feel like I'm falling apart," I begged James as he walked me towards the bar where people were meeting for pre-wedding festivities. Her death juxtaposed to my life at Cambridge left me hollow, crippled by guilt that I did not have the right to own against the realities of her life. He assured me, however, that I would be fine and we would meet back up very soon to go home.

I went through the rest of the night in rote motion, yet again. I drank and I smiled, and I did feel genuinely happy to see friends and acquaintances that I had not seen for years. I only shared what had happened with two close friends who were there that night. Two friends who I knew would understand the juxtaposition of happiness and sadness, swallowed up in the hands of a glass of wine. I drank away my pain that night and James came to get me as I sat staring out into the distance at a table where I felt a million miles away.

When I left my job teaching in Miami, I had taught the majority of my students for their first two years of high school. Many of them — including their parents — assumed I would see them all the way through high school, continuing to cycle through every grade level until graduation with them. We had all been through what felt like a lifetime together. So when I finally told them that I would be leaving the next year, going back to school to get my master's degree, I knew this decision would upset some students; but I was unprepared for the visceral reactions. While some said that they understood why I was leaving and that they believed I would go on to help other students, there were others who felt I was abandoning them, just as so many others had before me. I remember trying to explain my choice to one specific student, Martin, who had become like a son to me. He even referred to me as his 'mom' sometimes and stayed after school with me on most days.

"Martin, I have to leave so I can learn more, just as I want you all to continue learning long after high school," I tried again to explain to him.

"You don't *have* to leave. You *want* to leave," he angrily threw at me.

I had no words to say back to him. He was right, in a way, which is perhaps the only way that mattered in that moment. I did have a choice to stay, and I was choosing to leave. I, like so many others before, was abandoning him. As I reached out to him, he backed away from me and kept shaking his head, emphatically stating, "If you leave, I will never speak to you again." And he never has.

I am not arrogant enough to believe that I am the 'end all, be all' of my students' successes. Without me, most of them were fine. But there are those who you have a special bond with. The ones that you know in your heart need you around to help them back away from a grand precipice. I have heard since leaving that some of those students no longer attend the high school I taught at. They had been kicked out or sent to alternative schools. Schools that leave students with one foot in a classroom and the other foot on the streets. On days that were really hard during my year at Cambridge, I would ask myself if it would have been so hard to stay two more years? Would it have been so difficult to have seen those kids through until graduation? It hurts to live in the land of What-if. But it hurts even more to not be present. I had made a conscious decision to leave, and part of my journey of being at a place where I could be okay (if never perfectly okay) with leaving was acknowledging that the decision included hurting people I loved. Leaving was agreeing to some negative and adverse effects that may or may not trace back in part to my decision. On days that were really hard during my year at Cambridge, I also used this to fuel me.

I think of all of this and it draws me back to a night during my first term at Cambridge when I had dinner with two of my coursemates, Anthony and Natalie. I was expressing to them some of my mixed emotions about being at Cambridge; the sometimes sharp pangs of guilt I got when I thought about my classroom and my students.

"Why do you feel like that's your responsibility?" Natalie asked me as I finished talking.

I did not understand her question because I have always been a 'we' when it came to the collective work of survival and success. I do not attribute successes to single, brilliant instances that I orchestrated myself. I, one of the ones who did not die, am the sum total of all those who did die and for those who run head first into the street shielding me from the bullets.[69] I am one of the lucky ones, and with that luck comes an unspoken promise to be everything that I can be, do everything I can do, and create in ways yet unseen. Yet, she, in her white skin of acknowledged privilege, could not fathom such a situation, although she too had been a teacher for many years before going back to university.

But she had never been asked to represent her race in a group, nor had she ever been treated as if she possessed all 'prior knowledge' of those who looked like her. I do not dismiss the fact that there are different forms of being burdened; demons that appear in different shapes, with different faces. But in this regard, she had always been an individual—someone who failed and succeeded perceivably on her own neglect or prowess.

---

[69] A reference to June Jordan's work.

I have heard Natalie's question before, and sometimes from other black people themselves. During Lent term[70] I was feeling at my lowest, drained from the energy I put into my existence at the university and the failure to have it put back inside me. I longed for my amazing group of girlfriends from Miami, whom I could talk to about the things that plagued my mind as well as dance the night away, both featuring large bottles of delicious red wine. So I went looking for connection, for community, and stumbled across a group called FLY at an event my floormate Tabatha invited me to on intersectional feminism. The room was filled with a large diversity of women, and I instantly loved it. What I especially loved about the forum was that it was led by a black woman, and that women of colour featured the most in who talked, and the white women who were there listened. When the white women did talk, it was to add in relevant experiences and questions, never to trample on any of the experiences being shared by women of colour. Where had spaces like this been during Michaelmas?

I made sure to talk to Waithera, who was leading the event, and have her add me to the FLY Facebook group. I entered FLY at a time that it was really declaring what it was about, and asking those who did not fall under its sheltering umbrella to find other spaces to best serve their needs. FLY served as a safe space for both social and political engagement for BME women on campus. The majority of the women I met who were part of it were undergraduates. I saw so much of my own undergraduate self in them, especially in their frustrations of realizing how many walls ivory towers have built around themselves to keep the 'other' out.

FLY invigorated me. FLY wasn't about complaining; it was about women of colour at Cambridge recognising what we bring to these institutions, as well as what we must not allow them to take from us. It gave me a space to get back the energy I put out, and people to affirm

---

[70] Lent is the second term of Cambridge's calendar year. It lasts from roughly end of January to mid March.

my experiences with experiences of their own. It wasn't something I could always do with my white peers at Cambridge, although some were and are close friends of mine. (I have fond memories of mac n' cheese eating in ball gowns, long walks across meadows filled with reflection and laughter, pints of ale at English pubs, sunrise rows on the River Cam, and Edmund once saved my life.[71])

But the friends who got let into the complexities of my world were the ones who were willing to bear witness to it. At a Valentine's party I was co-hosting, my friend Brian started using what others referred to as a 'ghetto accent' in singing some rap songs. I was immediately turned-off by this minstrel show display and I called him out. As soon as I called him out though, I called him in to have a discussion on why it was not acceptable for him to do that and to ask where this was coming from. As soon as the encounter started, however, everyone else went away, and not because they wanted to give us privacy, but because I had done the cardinal sin of bringing up race and making those around me uncomfortable. Brian, though, stayed on that couch and had the conversation with me. Not to seek a 'cookie' for his Good White People gesture, but because he wanted to hear my thoughts— someone he knew and trusted—about matters he now understood the critical nature of engaging with, and would later put thoughts to action as well.

This was very different from individuals who would send me articles that they had already branded with all of their thoughts, simply telling me so I could give them the black girl nod of approval: You're a good white person, the BEST feminist. FLY was especially invaluable to me in the face of white feminism, which ran rampant on campus, stepping on the backs of women of colour like their ancestors before them. It is the type of feminism that comes with an 'acceptable' and 'unacceptable' brand that forces others to meet their requirements for capital F feminism[72] as Roxane Gay writes. Abu-Lughod refers to it as

---

[71] In a display of care I will never forget, Edmund stood between me and a charging bull during one of our many walks through Cambridge's numerous greens and meadows.

[72] Gay, Roxane. *Bad Feminist : Essays*. New York :Harper Perennial, 2014. Print.

as 'colonial feminism',[73] pointing to the exclusionary and forceful ways in which it builds up rules and exiles those who don't fit the mould. Should feminism not, however, be centred on the pursuit of liberation; to choose expressions of oneself? Why must one form of oppression be replaced with another? There is a vast difference between distancing oneself from whiteness (through the lens of one's feminism) and working toward dismantling it.

The solidarity amongst the women of FLY who pursued similar goals of what world we were working toward, reminded me of the collective work we do together. At one of the FLY events I attended, men of colour were invited to come and engage with us on a talk about the intersections of race, class and gender. It was a riveting conversation, one I was glad I could take part in, and it nourished me to know others were having these conversations on campus and thinking about these influences. One male questioned why it was our place to discuss these topics, such as the number of people of colour at Cambridge. He asked what would it take for us to be happy—more students of colour? More leadership and professors? Another voiced his concern of what happens when we become 'too political,' and that sometimes just 'being ourselves' and going about our business was the best response to institutional marginalisation and micro-aggressions.

I understand the fear of being labelled as the 'angry' or 'too vocal' minority in these types of spaces. Sometimes there are times when showing up and being excellent sends the message you want it to without uttering a word. Sometimes the weight of responding to every micro-aggression weighs down on my mental health and happiness. Being the person who gives voice to these issues can be an isolating and tiring position. And why should we have to? All this I recognise and acknowledge.

Then I locked eyes across the room with Anthony, a black man in my program, and he began to recount to the room times that black people

---

[73] Abu-Lughod, Lila. *"Do Muslim women really need saving? Anthropological reflections on cultural relativism and its others."* American anthropologist 104.3 (2002): 783-790.

had lifted him up to get him where he is, and the feeling that we are not meant to be here.

"I'll be damned if I don't use my position here to help others. None of us got here by ourselves," he declared, as he looked around the room.

I echo Anthony's words. His point has reverberated through my life. June Jordan reminds us that some of us did not die; some of us are still here despite the the hatred and violence that encircles us.[74] I am constantly—as I put it in my head– "in search of Martin." It is a complicated dance of having a platform but feeling guilty about the hands that hold me up. People who cannot see the "work" being done, but do the heavy lifting all the same. It also makes me reflect on how that guilt comes from my own complicated relationship with society's markers of success, and how we as the black community pursue them.

Through all the complexities, I am constantly trying to find practical and real ways to alter the spaces around me so that through my existence, I am not just being, but rather being in purposeful relation with others. I never want to leave a space and feel as though I did not contribute to it being a more decolonised, liberatory and revolutionary space for people of colour. That takes showing up and standing by the things I say, and living by those words as well. It takes seeing issues and finding ways to address them, knowing that real and substantial changes do not go to those who yell the loudest, but to those who are capable of crossing borders with the intention to cross back and blur the lines. And one day, just destroy them.

I used to avoid my teacher email account once I left Miami. I was frightened of the thought of reading emails that said how much a student missed me, and even more scared of the ones that asked me why I left. "Do you miss us, Ms. Younge? When are you going to come visit?" It is still a hard task, but at least in my moments of drawing from the strength being part of their lives has given me, I feel soothed by their

---

[74] Jordan, June. *"Some of us did not die: New and selected essays."* (2003).

in me. That I am still thinking about black children and black life. "Don't never stop being the best teacher." Those words have always spoken the loudest.

Dreams from My Mother

Waithera Sebatindira

I discovered a few summers ago how Barack Obama Sr. came to be in North America in 1959 – two years before the birth of his son in Hawaii. In that year, Tom Mboya, another Kenyan man and Oxford University graduate, set up a scholarship allowing underprivileged and academically gifted Kenyan students to study in the US. The scholarship has a number of very successful alumni, including Wangari Maathai, the first African woman to win a Nobel Peace Prize, and Obama Sr. I gushed to my mum about how incredible it was that Mboya had opened up so many opportunities for so many young people. Without hesitation, she responded saying: "Not even for them, think about what it's done for their children".

My mum's response reminded me of a FLY meeting where we discussed the pressure that comes with being the daughters of immigrant parents. While I don't qualify as such, I found that being raised for most of my life by a successful, single Kenyan mother raised similar issues, and I empathised with a lot of what was said.

A common feeling among members at the meeting was that we weren't just at Cambridge for ourselves. Rather, we were there for all the members of our family that contributed to our being there, and for those for whom our attending a university like Cambridge was a dream. Knowing this could be a burden. Most of us were already high-achievers who took low grades as a personal failure. Seeing this as us also failing those we love could seem unbearable. I could avoid this feeling most of the time (mainly by redefining success for myself in a way that didn't center academic work). But occasionally, while writing an essay that I knew was sub-par, I was reminded of my great-great-grandfather who, during a short visit to Cambridge in 1902, commented that he couldn't imagine anyone in his family ever being able to afford an education there. That was usually enough to get me off Netflix. But it was also enough to leave me drowning in guilt when my sub-par essay got me a suitably sub-par mark.

There was also the general awareness of the sacrifices that our parents had made, often for the sole purpose of giving their children the opportunities we'd gone on to take. I'll pause here to point out that I know that the stories of immigrant children and those of white, English working-class children will sound very similar. But it's hardly controversial to state that immigrants face a different struggle. One that's multi-faceted and more arduous. Specifically, the parents of first-generation migrant FLY members lack both white privilege and native privilege. This often means lacking class privilege, too. Rather than list the issues this can cause a person to face, I'll quote a nayyirah waheed poem instead:

> you broke an ocean in
> half to be here.
> only to find nothing that wants you.
>
>   – immigrant[75]

It's the case that few people, regardless of privilege, would be where they are without their parents or parental figures. But it's impossible to ignore the struggle of your parents when it's so painful, so tangible, and suffered almost entirely for your future. And knowing this, it then becomes difficult to not worry endlessly about that future being wasted. When your parents have "[broken] an ocean in/ half" you can't settle for just anything. Not meeting and exceeding your parents'

---

[75] Waheed, Nayyirah. *Salt* (2013). Print.

expectations can feel like a total lack of appreciation for what they've gone through.

It's not all doom and gloom, though. In fact, in this respect, I try not to see it as doom and gloom at all. It's stressful knowing how much rests on your shoulders, but it's also empowering. To know that you are part of something much bigger than yourself. That every step across King's Parade[76] is made possible by the dreams of family members generations before you. And I look forward to giving back as much as I can, as do the other FLY girls I spoke to. My mum often (half) jokes that I should pay for her early retirement. And to be honest, assuming I can get the right job I'll do that and more. Not just for her but, continuing in the tradition, for the children I hope to have myself. I'll continue to build on my future with the many privileges my mum's work has afforded me. Remember that she didn't push herself as hard as she did so I could settle for less than what a person in my position can achieve. Strive to make every Sebatindira who comes after me greater.

---

[76] King's Parade is a central street both in the city of Cambridge and within the University's campus. It lies outside King's College, one of the University's more famous colleges and is a historic feature.

The Muslim Woman's Burden

Suhaiymah Manzoor-Khan

Knowing that Cambridge was not only not what I thought it would be, but that it perpetuated the same systems that maintained the very establishment which sustained the very ideology that historically and currently broke the backs of my ancestors and people who looked like me, created a complicated relationship with a Cambridge education for myself and others with histories of British colonisation.

There was one evening where myself and few FLY girls started talking about the specific experience of being the child or grandchild of immigrants to Britain.[77] We all agreed that we were in the contradictory position where for our families, who had crossed continents to be here, we felt the euphoria of getting into Cambridge as if it were the culmination of an unspoken dream; yet for ourselves, we felt a lot of conflict and strife in being there. I remember the day I got my offer, my mother cried more about it than I ever have. Of course, most people are probably fairly pleased to get into Cambridge if they do, but for us FLY girls with migrant histories, we felt something more.

It is often the case that 'Western education' is prioritised by immigrants - especially as something they long for their posterity to acquire. In the case of migrants from ex-colonies, this is perhaps because of the history of colonialism which partially maintained power over the colonised through deprivation of literacy and other forms

---

[77] The same evening mentioned by Waithera in the previous chapter.

of knowledge, as well as through ideologically positing the 'superiority' of the coloniser and their language as one based on intellect and 'enlightenment' which the colonised lacked. Though false, the value of a British education was consequently widely internalised. Viewed as one of the best and most well-reputed educational institutions in the 'Western world', a Cambridge offer subsequently signified much more than a personal achievement to many of us. Rather than an 'I've made it' feeling, accessing such a privileged place of education felt like a 'we've made it'. We carried the hopes and dreams of those before us on our backs.

This was a very specific burden and one which made our existences at Cambridge feel somewhat revolutionary for us and those who we came from. However, that very particular and meaningful feeling of joy was balanced out by the feeling of actually being here. The profound alienation that could come with being simultaneously invisible and all too visible at Cambridge often counteracted the feeling of 'achievement'. We faced the contradiction of trying to educate ourselves out of a system engrained with imperialist, Eurocentric, patriarchal, 'secular' discourses and values, whilst simultaneously being in it.

My relationship with Cambridge was consequently always complex and contradictory. Whilst it suffocated me, if I had never been there, I may never have been made aware of all the ways in which the world around me was trying to suffocate me. Whilst draining in its white-ness, had I not experienced it, perhaps I would not have really come into or become as politicised about being racialised. Through the campaigning, workshopping, event-planning and organisational work I did with others in FLY, the Women's campaign and BME campaign in particular, Cambridge was a place I learnt how to act, collaborate and work with others towards awareness-raising and resistance. Once you start being vocal, confident and angry though - once you start drawing attention to what makes you different - people want explanations. Not always in interrogative ways. Sometimes in friendly, curious, interested ways. From those who loved me I believe it was a genuine question of understanding, but from others I was less close too, it was often a form of voyeurism too.

When I performed my first ever spoken word poem in Cambridge's ADC[78] open-mic Speakeasy I remember being shocked – in both a good way and a bad way – about how easy, almost too easy, it had been to impress the audience. How readily the whitest of audiences lapped up my stories of difference. And I say that not in a cruel way. It was flattering, it was nice. I felt as if I was being able to open people's eyes to a world they had perhaps never even had a minute to think about or realise was real. But within this was the shock, the almost dizzying realisation that this was maybe the first time they were hearing these things. They were impressed. They voted me straight to second place. But I always wondered whether it was because I was a particularly strong writer/performer, or because the things I was saying were so new to them.

The first poem I wrote and performed was called *"Token"*. Crudely strung together, obvious, and now very cringe-worthy to me, it still seemed eye-opening to that particular audience:

> Female.
> Muslim.
> Asian.
>
> I am almost the very antonym of the 'average person',
> who's obtrusive normality defies defining.
> Of the 'he' in any anecdote, who requires no description.
>
> You know the one
> Straight.
> White.
> Male.

---

[78] A theatre in Cambridge.

At first, they encourage you up
the steps, the ladder
smiling.
You smile back
unaware that their smiles
are not for you.

They smile for what you represent.
What you represent to them.
A nice new cover photo for the school magazine.
An 'exemplar' story about 'diversity'.
A 'tick' in the box of 'inclusivity'.
An A3 poster picture for 'equal opportunity'.

You can never be just another number.
You get your own whole category.
More, I get three:

Female.
Muslim.
Asian.

I am almost the very opposite of the 'person' who requires no prefixes,
who's superiority we have swallowed and continue to choke on.

Every time my mouthful of a name spills over the boundaries of their
        lists – beaming multiculturalism,
Every time they've asked to use my picture to advertise
        the organisation,
Every time the news station was filming at school and they happened
        to stumble upon me,

My success could never be personal.
My story was never just mine.
My experiences?
They are symbols.
Symbols that criss-cross several tick-boxes:

Female. Muslim. Asian.

Muslim. Female. Asian.

Asian. Muslim. Female.

You may ask whether I am not just perpetuating the problem,
by complaining only within the boundaries of being a Female.
        Muslim. Asian.
But these are the boundaries within which my experiences have
        been confined.
The walls inside of which my life has been constructed.
The categories outside of which I have hardly been able to exist.

And it is hard
to talk about yourself in ways other than those that your existence has
        been defined by.

It is hard
when no politician fits the same categories as you,
when no celebrity,
no school teacher,
no sports-star,
no comedian,
looks like or fits the same confines.

It is hard to know that if you thus want to become
a politician,
a celebrity,
school-teacher,
sport-star,
comedian,
You will never be seen as merely that.

For you are the opposite of the faceless figures who fill
        those occupations.
You know the ones.

Instead, you have the burden of being so Other.
Of being Female.
Of being Muslim.
Of being Asian.

I will never have the freedom of 'he' in every children's story.
'they' in every news article.
'you' in every advertisement.

I will never have the privilege, the right, or the supreme power
of being merely me.

It was exciting. It was exhilarating to force people to hear my story,
force them to imagine what it was like to not find it so simple and
straightforward at Cambridge.

The more I spoke up about the burden of never being able to be an
individual, though, I also ironically became the representative and
representation of 'otherness' in many spaces. I somehow became the
person people had to look at when they mentioned anything to do
with race, or the go-to representative for any time Islam hit the
headlines. In a way it was more liberating than when I had erased

and silenced myself – I no longer felt invisible - but the more vocal I was about the burden of representation the more vulnerable I felt about my words and opinions being misconstrued and misrepresented.

The burden of being 'othered' is felt by all who are. But sometimes I think I have underestimated that burden itself. Sometimes I have not realised the significance of my brown face and covered hair, my actions and my words. The significance to those around me, that is. The burden of representation.

Sometimes when you are the only example of a brown Muslim woman in a place like a Cambridge college, you can become (unwillingly, unwittingly and non-consentingly) *the* example of a brown Muslim woman. This can at first seem fine. What of it? It is the nature of a place lacking diversity. But when you think about it, it is terrifying. If you weren't present, there would be no example. And fine as that may seem, when you one day realise the impact your very existence has on people's understandings of brown people, Muslim people and brown Muslim women, the enormity of the burden of your presence hits you.

It comes in dribbles and in floods. Through chatting to people in the cafeteria. Through mentioning you need to go 'pray' in the middle of others' pre-drinks. Through explaining why you wear hijab to your friends. Through becoming the point of contact for opinions on anything to do with the 'non-Europe' or 'non-Christian' world. Through becoming the inadvertent defender of 'Islamic Feminism' by simply understanding it. Through existing in spaces people never thought you could.

I know I am not overstating its importance, because I myself would not have considered it had people not told me. From friends who tell me that they have learnt so much about the world through hearing my experiences, to strangers asking me about Islam. For them, I am the only visible representation of it they can see. People ask me about their presumptions and perceptions and often tell me how talking to me has 'enlightened' them. That may sound lovely, an ego-boost in fact, but more often than not it is terrifying. Sure, we all learn things from one-another—good friendships are nurturing and educative—but this was different.

First, it was exhausting, but second it was scary. The implication was that if I hadn't been there to say the things, to do the things, to refute the generalisations or to not fit the stereotypes, then ignorant assumptions would remain unquestioned. This was scary in itself, yes, but also scary in the burden it put on my existence. In my actions I was never anonymous, I could not be intimately human. Instead I became the unasked representative for entire categories of people who identified in similar ways to the ways I might.

The time this was made clearest to me was in my final term at Cambridge when one of my friends casually commented that he wondered how many people at Cambridge would 'not know a Muslim person' had I not been there. To me the statement sounded too big and too absurd. But on second thoughts it also made an alarming amount of sense. I wondered for how many people, how many families and how many dinnertime conversations, I was the Muslim in the sentence, 'I know a Muslim who…' or 'There's this Muslim girl in my college/faculty/etc who…'

I also wondered and still do wonder how many of those people became or will become the 'expert' on Muslims in other scenarios based only on their experience of tenuously 'knowing' me. My best friend from home once mentioned something to me which made this apparent. Catching up on eachothers' lives in between university terms she told me about the ignorance of her peers at a different university in the UK. She said when the topic of Islam came up she often had to weigh in and refute, challenge and clarify ignorance and misunderstandings. She chuckled saying that her expertise relied heavily on her experience of being my friend.

That hit me.

Here was the burden articulated at its finest: entire discourses relied upon my existence. Of course there is value in knowing people who can challenge our generalisations, but it is troubling to think that without those people such generalisations may go unchallenged. Why must it rely on 'othered' people to exist in ways that defy the generalisations propagated by wider culture to make people first think? My frustrations and this burden reached the point where they almost completely drained me. I oscillated between feeling I should educate people, defend myself and question their prejudices and ideas; and feeling far too small and too tired and alone to do so. There was also the frustrating irony that people freely alternated between deeming me the 'representative' and 'exception' as it suited them, making any effort on my part feel strained and uncertain.

This is where FLY came in once more. It is only in solidarity with other people that you can fight such large-scale and long-term battles and find the strength to educate people – for instance through writing, creating, organising and collaboration. But for me, the time to educate others on some things had passed. It passed because I no longer saw the need to defend my existence and I no longer had the energy to justify my methods of survival.

Surrounded by those who did not share my experiences at Cambridge, it took energy and time to explain or justify myself – and often without much reward. My identity was up for debate, my feelings up for interrogation and my experiences used to feed the curiosity of those around me: to signify 'trends' or 'interesting examples'. Therefore, to decline to engage with or to educate those around me whose privilege – if unacknowledged – blinded them from accepting my reality, was a proactive way I took care of myself. A way of protecting my now unafraid-to-stand-out but exhausted-by-having-to-justify-it-self self. It was self-preservation.

Shipwreck

I see it with my eyes
it registers in my mind
and then
the feeling
of heaviness
dives deep down my throat
sinks through my lungs
and comes to
rest
shipwrecked on my heart

'12 dead in gun attack'
'New bomb threat'
'Sidney siege'
'Boston marathon'
'woman arrested'
'six men charged'
Muslim.
Muslim.
Muslim.

The shipwreck
thrusts itself
deeper down inside me
smashing
into my stomach.

And this is so wrong.
For this is before
I register the tragedy.
Before I absorb
the names
the faces.

This is the weight instead of
guilt by association.
No.
That's wrong, not guilt,
fear.
And not association but
distant, disconnected affiliation.

A horrible mixture of anger, shame, regret,
determination not to make a condemnation into an apology
        for my personhood,
resentment that they dared call themselves the same as me.
This jumble of despair that sits on my heart
this weight,
is from a mere word.

A word I dread to hear in these contexts,
but a word to which I associate
and yet have only some control over.

The others
countless others
all have some control
too
and yet
it is always the loudest who the mic will pick up.

You cannot seem to create meaning
through smiles,
or jokes,
or cups of tea.
Through working long hours,
or feeding your kids.

You can't seem to make meaning
through being a neighbour,
a school-friend,
a teacher,
the postman,
the doctor,
the parent,
even the victim.

Your claim to the word,
is not really noted if you only
work the till,
baby-sit on the weekends,
shop online,
take walks in the park,
pay off your mortgage,
or miss the last bus home.

Instead, meaning is controlled
through bangs and blood.
Through black, yellow, red,
a scream and a thud.

This weight is not made by the many.
The shipwreck is caused by the few.
And yet all of us,
everyone on board,
feels like they are drowning.

Where are All the Black Men?: The Painful Silence in Solidarity from Men of Colour

Waithera Sebatindira

During my second year at Cambridge, FLY held a meeting that hosted Cambridge's men of colour (MoC). The meeting as a whole was a success. A surprisingly high number of men turned up and, by the end of the meeting, conversation was spirited and flowing freely. But it's important to discuss the reason why we felt the need to host men.

The numbers that attended were surprising because until then, it had always appeared that MoC at Cambridge were politically apathetic. From the 2013 "I, Too, Am Cambridge"[79] campaign to panel discussions on racial politics, it had predominantly been women of colour at the forefront of anti-racist activism at Cambridge.

We'd hoped at the meeting to get to the bottom of this gender disparity, and a lot of interesting opinions came to light. There were two arguments that interested me most: 1) the idea that it's not our responsibility as people of colour to help other PoC; and 2) the idea that academic and professional success will prevent us from experiencing racism. These opinions are understandable but misguided.

I'll begin with the second point because I empathise with it most. Going to the sort of private school where I was the only black person in my year for three years running, I thought the best way forward was to ignore my race and let my grades do the talking. After all, if we all

---

[79] http://wetooarecambridge-blog.tumblr.com/

156

had the same educational advantages, I surely had nothing to complain about. But my Cambridge offer never stopped staff from following me around in high street shops. Our degrees won't stop police violence, or protect us from job discrimination against white people with the same qualifications. Won't protect our children from being teased for their funny names and funny skin. We can't outrun racism with respectability politics. More importantly, as human beings we deserve basic respect simply for existing. We shouldn't have to collect Firsts in return for our humanity being recognised by our peers and by the state. Yes, money and a great education will protect us from many manifestations of racial prejudice. But if we want to end racism we have to fight racism itself, not pretend that we can place ourselves outside of its grasp.

The question of whether it's our responsibility to help other PoC is easier to deal with. It is our responsibility. It's unfair that that's the case, but we have our places at Cambridge because of activists before us who refused to accept the status quo. We didn't ask for their help and they didn't hand us a literal baton. But if we're interested in a world of success that's accessible not only to us but to everyone, opening doors for others is what we have to do.

This doesn't explain why it appears to be the case that MoC at Cambridge are more inclined to buy into these arguments than WoC. This wasn't fully addressed at the FLY meeting but, at least in my mind and in the context specifically of black men, there is one clear reason why there are more women activists: the ease with which a lot of black men are able to assimilate into environments like Cambridge.

Anecdotal and empirical evidence shows that black boys in predominantly white schools have an easier time (than black girls) as-similating because of the stereotypes associated with black men.[80] This remains the case when those black boys grow up and enter university. While there are no genuinely positive stereotypes of black men, it's

---

[80] Aboubacar Ndiaye, 2013. *Black Boys Have an Easier Time Fitting In at Suburban Schools Than Black Girls.* [online]

easy to see how the idea that black men embody "coolness", for example, can make it easier to integrate - even to become popular. This in conjunction with the fetishisation of black men (case in point: the anonymous straight woman who allegedly filled in her RAG blind date form[81] saying she was looking for an "afro-exotic experience") means acceptance is that much easier. It explains why black men might, therefore, be less inclined to rock the boat by joining controversial campaigns that would other them from their white friends. Moreover, assimilation can look a lot like equality, leading to assumptions among black men that there is, in fact, no need for said campaigns.

The same evidence shows that black girls (and women) are only hampered not helped by the stereotypes held against us. Tropes that class us as inherently loud and unattractive malcontents are unlikely to earn us many new friends. Yet even if seemingly positive stereotypes about us did exist, I personally can't see the benefit of using them as a foundation for assimilation (nor would I want to assimilate at all). Moreover, it's clear that assimilation is not the same thing as equality when your white friends engage you in plainly racist "banter". When a stark educational attainment gap continues to persist between black and white students[82]. When you've been stopped and searched by police officers after a night out and none of your other friends are even aware that things like that happen in a place like Cambridge.

More than anything, it's painful to think that those who should be our closest allies— those whose liberation is inseparably tied to our own — would leave us to carry out the work of liberation. My own experience has seen black men be far more likely to publicly criticize

---

[81] RAG stands for "raising and giving". It is a university society committed to engaging students in fundraising for charitable causes. Once a year, they organise university-wide blind dates around Valentine's Day for which students have to donate £5 (at the time of writing) to participate. Each participant fills in a form detailing their interests before they're assigned to another participant for a blind date. Assignments are made randomly, although if you donate more money you can specify what sort of person you would like to be paired with.
[82] https://www.varsity.co.uk/news/13963

anti-racist activism at Cambridge to much white approval. Quite frankly it feels like a betrayal, and it's one that's seen on a national level as well. "Stop killing the mandem"[83] became a popular tagline for Black Lives Matter (BLM) activism in London, while the movement in the US consistently focuses on male lives lost. Given the strides I've seen Cambridge take following the agitating of black women, it seems black men are having their cake and eating it, too: they can distance themselves from the controversy of activism while also reaping the benefit of its successes.

It's frustrating as well. While co-organising the Black Lives Matter solidarity campaign after Darren Wilson was acquitted, it was incredibly difficult to get black men involved. Myself and the co-organiser (also a woman) knew that black women had to be involved, but we also knew that the constant focus in the media on cishet black men[84] meant we had to have black men photographed as well. One or two were keen from the beginning, but most had to be directly contacted and asked to contribute. This felt weird given that the movement was implicitly known to centre black men and that we'd done all the work organising – all they had to do was show up. This level of disengagement worried me. If black men had this much difficulty showing up when black women organised for them, would they ever show up for us in the future?

What was particularly telling was the response when this piece was published online on the Fly. blog. Comments underneath (and underneath a sister-piece written specifically about brown men) ranged from patronising claims that WoC are overly sensitive to outright indignation. Never before had I seen MoC speak so passionately about racial politics, yet it was in defence of their own apathy. The existence of structural racism was denied, lived experience dismissed as "childish and juvenile complaints". A demand was made that WoC be even more patient than they already are in educating

---

[83] https://www.complex.com/life/2016/07/black-lives-matter-london-dallas-protest-july-8
[84] Cisgender and heterosexual black men.

MoC. We were called "divisive".

How so many men seem to prefer to ignore what's staring them right in the face and instead play pretend-post-racial-Britain is beyond me. A black female friend of mine at another prestigious British university was involved for some time in anti-racist activism and eventually declared that she was done organising for MoC. I can see why, sometimes. All of that being said, I do not believe that white Cantabrigians only befriend black men because they hold certain stereotypes about them. Nor am I saying that fitting in among white people automatically makes it more difficult to engage with these issues. This is less about the relationships we have with each other, and more about the possible effect those relationships can have on our political beliefs. The trends I've noted above exist and are known to exist. They contribute to the extent to which black men are able to assimilate into the Cambridge student population, which may then affect their decisions to get involved in campaigns calling for racial equality. This is not the case for all black men, and I don't know whether it's the case for MoC as a whole. Black men can and do experience difficulty assimilating into some environments. I'm also not saying that politically active black women are only active because they feel excluded at Cambridge.

Finally, I should note that MoC at Cambridge aren't completely apathetic. 'SAW' is a network that was set up a few years ago with the specific aim of creating solidarity and a shared space for MoC (much like FLY). The alumni who established the group saw that there are conversations that MoC need to be having at Cambridge. Though SAW has become less well-known over the years, it has recently been revived, which hopefully marks the beginning of better engagement with race politics from MOC at Cambridge.

To Cambridge's MoC: We know that there is work to be done by PoC of all genders. You don't have to take to the streets or become your college access officer. Accepting that assimilation isn't equality is the best first step. Call out your friends, join SAW, begin to address the fact that we aren't fully equal and that isn't our fault. All of us, with our immense educational privilege, have the power to change the future for the better. Not simply for ourselves, but for others like us as well.

PART SIX:
Intersectionality

i am hurting for sisters whose pain i will never have to bear.
the strength to carry that weight – only love is left alive.

-

pop bead metaphysics sounds like a game for kids –
humanity cordoned off, entering in single file.
ballot-boxes of identity; I do not speak in colour –
nor can I see without it.

-

we meet on different roads. your sisters are hers
are hers are hers are hers are hers are mine.

-Jun Pang

From Overwhelmed to Empowered
Odelia Younge

But the horror of that moment stays with me, the realization that being smart and working hard might never be enough. I wasn't sure how I could survive a world that would constantly question my abilities, give me more obstacles than my peers, and then downplay my achievements when I somehow managed to deliver. I was overwhelmed by the thought of having to be a black girl for the rest of my life.[85]

–Khadijah White

When I was about 9 years old, I auditioned to be the lead in the school's holiday play. I was determined to get the role and fervently practiced all the lines. I gave it my all when the auditions came about and many of my classmates told me what a great job I had done. But I didn't get the lead role. In fact, I didn't get any visible role. The lead went to a new girl with bouncy blonde hair and blue eyes. When I asked the music instructor if she did not think I had done a good job, she said, "It's not that…it just wouldn't have looked right."

At age 9 I had encountered enough moments of overt and passive racism to know that what she meant was that I, the lone black girl in a sea of white faces, would have been 'alarming' as the lead in a Christmas play. Years later I realised that she could not comprehend

---

[85] Khadijah White, *"Racism affects black girls as much as boys. So why are girls being ignored?"* Washington Post, 2015.

me existing in such a space. Even before I possessed the words to describe what was happening to me in my world and in my mind, I still felt it deeply. I often wondered if it would be that way for the rest of my life.

My only solace was in the centre of my universe – my home, where my mother did not raise any self-hating children. There, within those four walls, I could at least have my humanity affirmed, receive rejuvenation and support, and not look for my acceptance in spaces not ready or wishing to do so. My mother's greatest fear each day as she sent us off to school was not about our failure. No, she always knew we would excel academically. Her greatest fear was that people would attempt to cut us down, to make us feel as though we we were inferior and did not belong.

My mother had a great love of reading. All of us children were reading abridged versions of thick novels by the time we were in first grade. Books were precious to me. They allowed me to expand the limited knowledge I was given in school, and learn about different ways of being, and the different faces of brilliance. Through the writing in books I saw myself, and those worlds fed me. They turned the alienated thoughts of a young black girl into shared feelings. I was never alone.

As I grew older I felt the intersection of my race and gender more. There was a perverse boldness that allowed a male friend of mine to declare to another close friend of ours that he would date me if I were white. I was also constantly bombarded with images that excluded me from standards of beauty. My black wasn't the 'acceptable' black. My beauty not falling within the lines of 'beige bombshells.'

"Somebody, anybody, sing a black girl's song." [86]

I refuse to choose sides for those who require it. My concerns with race issues do not negate any connections with the specific trials of

---

[86] Shange, Ntozake. *For Colored Girls Who Have Considered Suicide When the Rainbow Is Enuf: A Choreopoem*, New York: Collier Books, 1989. Print.

being a woman. I often say I 'advocate feminism', as bell hooks says, because the current feminist movement is still stifled by the inability to recognise the unique intersections of women of colour. Feminism as an identity lends itself to preconceived notions of who can represent that work.[87] I feel the weight and lifting of my race and gender like the ebb and flow of the ocean tides, and drinking from that ocean quenches my feelings of being overwhelmed for the rest of my life.

But that ocean is often a dangerous flow, currents fast and sometimes treacherous. We must be careful in our engagements with binary identities that we gain no protection from; identities that society does not attribute to our lives in the same way as others. There are white damsels in distress, and pregnant black women chained to beds to give birth. My friend Jonathan Jacob Moore writes, "I think often about what it means to raise a black person with the consciousness that gender will be used throughout their life to normalize the violence they experience and reaffirm a subjecthood, a right to life, a right to being, that they simply don't have in this world.[88] Yet, my chosen identity as a black woman, once defined by myself, has given me communities that call me their own and has informed me of which communities are not for me. It is through this identity that I best understand the movements of the ocean.

Anthony, the only black man in my program who later became a good friend of mine at Cambridge, started out as someone I was in constant struggle with. On the night we forged a friendship, he asked me why it was that we had encountered such a deep rift between us. I told him I could remember distinct moments in class and in conversation when I would offer my thoughts on a topic and I could feel him mentally shut me off, sometimes physically rolling his eyes and turning away, as if to say that I had nothing of value to add.

He had dismissed me.

---

[87] Hooks, Bell. *Feminist Theory: From Margin to Center*, Cambridge, MA: South End Press, 2000. Print.

[88] Excerpt from a Facebook post.

Here was a black man who had fallen headfirst into the historical trench of too many black men not showing up to uphold the right to life of their sisters. And I felt that because he was a black man, it had opened the door for others to treat me that way as well. I could feel myself drowning in a thick smog of the need to be heard and to have my voice counted. I would enter the classroom for meetings of my program, ready with comments and engagement with the reading, but leave without uttering a word. Most conversations were dominated by the same white men in the course — a course of only four men, I should state — who were men who had been taught over the years that their thoughts had disproportionate value. I could see the lecturers defer to their comments and their questions (some they answered themselves after posing), and they would speak without waiting to be acknowledged. They would interrupt or make points that were already mentioned. Just bolder and more assured. It was like I was desperately trying to learn the ten words that Soraya Chemaly wrote every girl should learn:

"Stop interrupting me."

"I just said that."

"No explanation needed."[89]

Chemaly goes on to state, "Socialized male speech dominance is a significant issue, not just in school, but everywhere. If you doubt me, sit quietly and keep track of speech dynamics at your own dinner table, workplace, classroom." That's precisely what I started doing. I started quietly noting or tally marking on paper when it happened. I wasn't surprised at what my crude experiment found. And while this caught me in a war with myself and with others, it was the lack of engagement with points I made, whether inside or outside of class, that was most inexcusable to me.

I remember one specific moment when the conversation turned to the work of Michael Young. I had researched Michael Young for my first

---

[89] Soraya Chemaly, *10 Words Every Girl Should Learn*, Huffington Post, 2014.

literature review of the course, as I wanted to critique his arguments in my essay. The lecturer that day loosely summarised some of Young's ideas and did not give them enough time. I felt this was an injustice to the conversation, as I find Young's work disturbing and slightly sinister in its deepest notions; so I raised my hand to bring up a point questioning what he meant when he etched the phrase 'powerful knowledge.' I voiced concern that he was using old 'blame the victim' tactics. He was suggesting that if disadvantaged students were to learn the skills he believed were the only ones worth learning, they would be as powerful as others in society. This, without any regard to external factors or structural barriers. It also shut down discourse analysis. Kurt—one of the males in the class—nonchalantly stated that if Young was encouraging others to pursue knowledge as the end goal of schooling, then he didn't see anything wrong with that.. I could tell Kurt had never truly engaged with the writings of Young, yet believed his opinion to be on par with that of someone who had done their homework, and I looked at him—rocking back in his chair, with his pen in his mouth—and said, "That is NOT what Young meant."

His only response was to shrug his shoulders and look away from me.

Dismissed.

The lecturer moved on as if none of it mattered or had ever occurred.

This was my academic life: I had to reassert myself in the classroom, and not back down in moments when I knew I had something of value to add; and I refused to let others diminish my experiences or silence my voice. A week after the Michael Young conversation, Young himself came to Cambridge to give a talk through the Faculty of Education. The lecturer from that class was the one in charge of the group who was putting on the event. Young was everything I imagined he would be. He was pompous and bold in speech. He shut down ideas of children learning differently as nonsense, and said nothing was as important to learn as the disciplines white men in the past set out for the rest of us. To their credit, many in the audience from the faculty pushed back against his notions in their questions. But this was *after* he had been invited to talk.

I sat there taking the entire scene in. After the event, I went up to Young to introduce myself and tell him about what I found as I researched his work. Anthony and I went up to him together, and although I was clearly the one interested in his research, he deferred all his answers and conversations to Anthony.

Dismissed.

After the talk, Anthony, myself, and one other person from our course went to dinner with two of our lecturers, including the one from the Young conversation incident. Throughout much of the dinner she lamented having played a part in allowing a man such as Young to come talk for a group that was supposed to be about educational equity.

"I didn't know much about his work. I had no idea he was going to talk about things like that," she explained.

I could not help myself, as I slipped in, "That's what I was trying to explain in class that day."

None of this truly surprise me. I was the voice least likely to be validated. My opinions were nodded at for liberal satisfaction, yet swiftly pushed aside. It was almost as if to say, "Thank you for your input, but we have it from here". And therein lies the tension: the hyper-examination that comes with excelling and the hyper-examination that comes with my assertion of my presence, both coupled with the need to dismiss me as an anomaly, the exception.

I am hyper-visible and hyper-invisible all at once. I have a deep fear of drawing too much attention to myself, and a deep fear of being 'dismissed' and ignored. Even when I thought I had carved out space for myself at Cambridge, there would come a reminder that I was not supposed to be there, and in many ways, was not wanted in the ways I dared to show up. One night during the winter recess, that came in the form of the ability of others to dismiss my statements and brand me me the offender.

It was New Year's Eve and my friend Courtney and I had plans to bring in the new year. We bought tickets to a 1920s party which we attended until after midnight, when the venue's population of men who were there escaping their girlfriends and wives became too overwhelming and strange. We set our sights down the road to a club we had been to on many Friday nights with our college, so we had no worries we would not be let in. When we arrived there was no line so we were shocked when the bouncer refused to let us in. He was a large, bald man with an unfriendly face, who would not look us in the eye. He asked us to wait in a non-existent line. We waited. Minute after minute passed and others came behind us and were let in. After a while I asked him why he would not let us in. He said it was because we were drunk. We had been drinking earlier in the night, but our last drink was quite some time ago and we were in no worse or better shape than anyone else going inside the club. I approached him to explain that we were fine, and as I did so, he lashed out and pushed me—hard. I tripped and fell back; Courtney and I were both shocked, and Courtney began calling a relative who was a police officer, and I tried calling out to the female bouncer, hoping she would empathize with me in solidarity that even if I was not allowed inside the club, I should not be touched by this man. She ignored me. She turned her head and ignored me.

Dismissed.

My right to comfort as a black woman in the face of what was now two men blocking my path and one that had physically shoved me, was not important to her. When the police arrived, I was relieved it was a female officer. She approached me and told me I had to leave. I asked her why, trying to force her to look me in the eye, but she would not. I asked her to watch the video footage from the club to see him shove me, and she said she did not need to. I asked her to breathalise me, she said she did not need to. At that, the little piece of myself that still cracks when faced with others' inability to see and hear me, cracked even more. I felt my eyes swell up, and as the first tears hit my face, I hated the begging voice that arose from my chest and pleaded, "Why won't you even entertain the fact that I might be telling the truth? That I might be the victim?"

But the law does not protect me in the ways it protects other women. At no point in all of this was Courtney treated the same. She noticed this too and started to ask the bouncers and the police officer why they were treating me like this, telling them that I was never in trouble and belonged to Clare College. I repeated that I was a student at Clare, as if my institutional affiliation would somehow change their views about me. KNOW ME! RECOGNIZE ME! As if to say, I was one of the "good ones." But there are no 'good ones' and 'bad ones'. Just ones. And I knew that.

As Courtney continued to demand an answer to why they were treating me like this, and if it was because I was black, the police officer told Courtney that she had one minute to remove me from the premises or she would remove us herself, and possibly take us into custody. I stood there defeated and unmoving until Courtney's arms were tightly around my shoulder, leading me away from the club. I started sobbing as we walked away, repeating over and over again: It doesn't matter, Courtney. I told her that it didn't matter where I was, whether it was back home or thousands of miles across the ocean, because I would always be treated by some as a second-class human. To many, I would always just be another *nigger*.

I am the face of people's fears, whether I am on the street or in a lecture hall. Even amongst those I count(ed) as friends, there have been stinging moments and subtle reminders that you are not one of us. Some people cannot recognise how exhausting it is to reside in spaces that were not meant for people like me, and how often black women are forced into those spaces. There is the constant need to validate that existence, especially when such validation may lead to survival. But at what cost to oneself?

It is even more painful to have people make you feel institutional barriers on a personal level. The constant reminder of outsider status. I was and am grateful for Courtney's presence that night. She never left, and kept her hands held tightly around my shoulder, crying with me, while allowing me to feel every bit of pain from that moment. I may not believe in the way we frame allyship, but I do believe in presence: sitting in the realities of an anti-black world.

There's been a movement of famous blacks–many entertainers—calling themselves part of the New Black who believe that race and racism do not matter anymore. I often wonder what happens, not necessarily when these individuals meet with society at large, but rather when they encounter themselves. I feel for them. To have stripped yourself of the very legacy that has made us today. Being black is me and it has empowered me.

After years of feeling overwhelmed and afraid of being silenced, I have found power in discomfort, as I discussed in an interview for a blog piece with another teacher in Miami. Catherine said, "In college, I was in intense classes and forward thinking conversations, and I realized I was different than other people. I never knew the discomfort when you realize that you are the only person in a room that isn't white or only person who is female and speaking and sharing ideas. In that kind of discomfort, you gain power because you realize that you have important things to say. And because I have things to say because of my experiences, I have an authority to speak on issues, and should be speaking on them. With my voice I should be allowing those without a voice to have a place to speak as well."

I am grateful in many ways, for learning the lessons of discomfort at a young age. I am a walking litany for survival, and I have survived because and for those who cannot indulge in the passing dream of choice, and those who were imprinted with fear from birth. As Audre Lorde stated, I have found that it has been better to speak as one who was not meant to be here–not meant to survive.[90]

---

[90] Audre Lorde, "A Litany for Survival", in Lorde, *The Black Unicorn.*

I could cower in a corner. I could build my life in 'approved' spaces and ways, wielding personal success as the end all of success. I could choose to exist solely in relation to institutions of power.

What I have chosen instead is to exist for the sake of my own humanity. I have chosen to live to push the boundaries of discomfort, and to recognise that gaining access without intent to disrupt would be my own complicity in systems of oppression. Being a life-giver for yourself and others is an active choice. We know that social justice issues do not get addressed out of nowhere. That's why we need the FLY organisations of the world. We have to actively and consciously make things happen.

I realised that is why I write. Not just chronicles of my life, but works of fiction as well. I started writing at a young age to create spaces for myself where I and people who looked like me could also exist. After all, one of the first steps is imagination; the ability to do what my music teacher so long ago was incapable of doing: widening and re-imagining the narrative. And when I find myself in spaces where the walls threaten to close around me — spaces that dare to silence me — I think about the words of Assata Shakur:

> *And, if I know anything at all,*
> *it's that a wall is just a wall*
> *and nothing more at all.*
> *It can be broken down.*[91]

[91] Shakur, Assata. (1987/2001), *Assata: An Autobiography*, (Chicago: Lawrence Hill Books), p.1

Sandra Bland

I dip my toes into some of the clearest blue waters I have ever encountered.

I look down and see the outline, the shadow of a woman.

I am safe here, yet I am haunted by the rough hands of police officers and a mugshot that is a death shot. Not even the final moment, but an image of life that has long exited from her body.

I am safe here. Yet what is safety?

I dive into the clear blue water, eyes stinging from the rush of salt water, body rocking with the waves of the sea.

And the sky is cloudless. It is not marred by a single cloud. Its expanse is as far reaching as I could ever imagine.

I am safe here, yet I am haunted.

I hear the echo of voices spitting out that SHE DESERVED TO DIE. That her arrogance ended her life. Nothing more. Nothing else.

As a black woman, there is arrogance in being alive. Arrogance in owning your body, making your own spaces. Being too fly while sharpening your oyster knife to mind the shadows lurking up behind you to take it all away in a single moment.

I am safe here, yet I am haunted.

I sit down on slippery rocks while the waves crash over my body. I close my eyes and recite Lorde from memory. "Call me roach and presumptuous/ nightmare on your white pillow"

Say her name.

She should haunt you too.

- Odelia Younge

Doing Womanhood as a Black Person

Waithera Sebatindira

Every International Women's Day at universities across the UK, a
'Reclaim The Night' [92] (RTN) march is organised by feminist groups.
Women march through public spaces at night, chanting about their
right to personal autonomy and confidence while occupying said
spaces. I love seeing women all over the country demand safe access
to their cities and neighbourhoods, both during the night and the
day. It's important that there's an accessible event whereby women
and groups that face structural misogyny can publicly address the fact
that they're less safe than men are on streets that should belong to all
genders in equal measure.

That being said, 'Reclaim the Night' is also a complicated event for me.
The solidarity among all the women taking part is particularly heartening, but therein lies a potential problem. We're all drawn together by
our collective experiences but, as is often the case wherever marginalised groups are called together, the intersections of other oppressions
are often ignored. As a black woman, I feel the exact same fear that a
white woman feels while walking the streets alone at night, but there's
more to my experience than there is to hers.

The scene: I am walking back to my college accommodation late at
night. The badly-lit road is empty but for the occasional speeding car.

---

[92] Reclaim the Night marches began being held in the UK in 1977. They are usually
organised on the Saturday closest to 25th November, which marks the UN Day to End
Violence Against Women.

I come across a white woman who is very, very drunk. She's crouched on the ground, on her own, swaying slightly, very vulnerable. I stop and, without touching her and while maintaining my distance, ask if she needs help. I ask if she lives near here and if her friends know where she is. She's unresponsive until I offer out my hand for her to hold on to. She then begins to laugh and repeat over and over "You're not allowed to do that. You're not allowed to do that to me." While I'm trying to figure out how to help her, a car suddenly drives off the road beside us. It stops and a white man comes running towards us. He stops, ignoring me completely, and asks the woman, "Is everything OK here?" As she doesn't respond, I ignore the fact that the question wasn't directed at me and explain the situation. He walks straight up to the woman and asks again if she's alright, at which point she raises up both of her arms pleadingly and says, "Help me."

I left him to it. Neither bitter, nor angry, not even surprised. Because it's happened before. In fact, it happens quite often. White women who view me with fear on the street, be it night or day. Those who give me a wide berth or clutch their purses and children closer to them when I walk past. There is no solidarity for me with all women when I walk the streets at night, because I know that to some of them I am one of the threats that they have to navigate while trying to get home. Never mind that I too live with their fear. Like all women, I struggle to know how to react when catcalled in the middle of the night. A nervous (terrified) smile might be interpreted as an invitation. Ignoring it might incur their wrath. The freedom to roam without the fear of attack is also withheld from me. I need 'Reclaim the Night' just as much as any other woman.

Adding to this complexity is the strange experience of being feared by men as well. On public transport they draw their briefcases to their chest. I've had men walk off of the pavement into the middle of the road to avoid walking by me. It is strangely offensive. My fear of them is symptomatic of the rape culture in which we live where sexual harassment and violence against women is the norm. Their fear of me is purely racist.

This fear goes beyond offence, though. White people's fear is terrifying because of the consequences it can incur. I fear that white people's fear will lead to a call to the police – an arm of the state that kills black people with impunity. My feminism is necessarily anti-carceral because should I face gendered violence on our streets, there is no world in which I could turn to the criminal justice system as so many mainstream feminists advocate. White people's fear in itself is used to police my existence in public spaces, as scared and hateful stares cause me to shrink myself and treat myself like a criminal, keeping my hands where they can be seen and my eyes to the ground. I genuinely worry about random acts of violence from white people who might perceive me as a threat. I don't know that I would be treated with sufficient leniency should I ever need to defend myself from a hate crime, as the assumption is always that people that look like me are the aggressor.

This is all to say that intersectional discussions of women's safety at night are needed. I know why it's so easy for white women to divorce my womanhood from my blackness, and focus on what, to them, is a threat. I get that simply writing about it won't change their hurtful and potentially dangerous perceptions. I also understand that 'Reclaim the Night' isn't purely about our safety at night, and that my focusing on this one issue alone may seem to evince a confused, over-simplified interpretation of the event's purpose.

Conversations on this are important regardless, because silencing them in spaces such as RTN only serves to maintain those spaces as existing solely for the comfort of white women. They're inevitably uncomfortable and that tension is essential to the work of liberation for ALL women. This includes trans women who suffer astounding levels of violence on these streets, and whose gender should never be policed on an RTN march (or ever). Queer women who feel unable to hold hands with their partners on these streets. Homeless women who are forced to live on these streets. Women who are unable to march due to disability or caring responsibilities, and whose commitment to liberation should not be questioned. Every woman who exists outside the imagery of mainstream feminism's "typical" woman.

I'm hoping that future conversations about solidarity among women will truly include the experiences of all women. It's a very basic call to intersectionality, but it's not one I've heard talked about often enough: the contradiction of living as both threat and threatened. It's exhausting having to fear some of the people I meet on the street while also considering the fact others on the street fear me. I know there must be other black women — tall and apparently intimidating women — who share these feelings. We need more opportunities to discuss them.

When They Find You Unpalatable and Abrasive, that is When You're Doing It Right

Suhaiymah Manzoor-Khan

Sorry

We mumble 'sorry' as a mantra
whilst negotiating our existence
'Sorry' you almost knocked Me over
'Sorry' you sat in My way
'Sorry' you held the door open for Me
'Sorry' you elbowed My ribs.

We were taught to apologise.
Taught our existences were a favour.
Every inch we took up was borrowed spaced.
Every time we left the house was a show.

Be presentable

palatable

placid

peaceful.

Exist, but only in a confined way.
Survive, but only with rasping breath.

We apologise as if our bodies are playthings
as if our beings are not ours.

We are not art work
waiting to be appreciated.
You can't hang us up
or tie us down.

But they do.

Tie us up by our hair
Rake our eyelashes back
Pull our stomachs in
Rip our follicles out
Paint our smiles on.

'Sorry' we say
when we forget to be tied down.

Apologising for existing
in ways unacceptable.

Apologising that life is messy
that the media is perverse
and that obstacles are our path.

We tiptoe, some of us
'Sorry' for existing too much.
Being Too Big.
Too Small.
Too Black.
Too White.
Too Naked.
Too Covered.

You may own your space
but at a price:
that you swallow your soul whole.

We teach boys to live
and we teach girls to just survive.
We tell the others they must not exist.

We say 'learn to hurt'
Learn to carry pain
like stones in your pockets
so that by the time you're at school
your child's skirt
is weighed down low enough
to teach you the shame
that is your body.

We teach girls that it is always best to hurt.
Always best to settle for less.
We teach them
that the only way to see themselves
is in the eye of the beholder.

They know the beholder.
Know his tastes
because he ejaculates them
over every magazine
every advertisement, screenplay and song.

So we tell our babies labelled Girl
to live always in the cornea of a gazing man.
No.
The cornea of every man.

We teach boys to live
And we teach girls to survive
From the day we label babies
We begin to wage a war.

A war only some of us apologise for.

I find that the person I never apologise to
is me.

War weary and unacceptable
I get stuck in people's teeth
and make them squint their eyes.

'Sorry'
But this time I say it to myself.
'Sorry' they tried to hold you down.
'Sorry' you believed they should.
'Sorry' that you believed they could.

Vomit your soul back up.
Violently
Lovingly
Messily.

Do not be sorry to exist.

The second way FLY changed my experience at Cambridge was by introducing me to radical black feminists such as Audre Lorde, Patricia Hill Collins, bell hooks, and Angela Davis. I devoured their works over the Christmas vacation of my second year, having never before even considered why mainstream feminism had made me uncomfortable. I was overjoyed to learn it was not me who was the problem, but that there were whole generations of women before me who were critical of 'The Feminist Movement'[93]. I felt exhilarated to learn why talk of sexism which ignored racism, and racism which ignored sexism ignored my experience as someone who existed at the intersection of both. I felt dismayed to learn how integral imperialist discourses were in Western feminism and uplifted to learn that I should be wary of all who tried to define my liberation for me.

And yet, as much as the women of FLY and these books on black and intersectional feminist work fed my thirst, I found myself increasingly yearning for information more specifically about me. For the explanation of and theories on 'South Asian' women; of the context of Britain rather than the USA, and specifically of the British Empire, Islam and the way Muslims have been constructed historically. I longed for analysis of the intersection where my identity lay.

To see the relevance of European colonialism, the history of the slave trade and the experience of slavery for black women's experiences of racism and sexism was essential. Yet I could not claim their history as my own. Our oppressions had specific and different contexts which I needed to find out. Subsequently, in my quest to learn about my own circumstances and my need to know my own history, I began to shape my academic pursuits around these personal desires: towards finding the writers and women who could speak directly to and of me.

As the grandchild of migrants to Britain — migrants coming from 'The Empire' to the 'Imperial Metropole'— being in academia and having the opportunity to research aren't trivial matters. When the

---

[93] Referring to the mainstream western-centric feminism usually chartered into a trajectory of waves from 'suffrage' claims in the early 1900s to a 'second wave' in the 1960s and so on.

time came to choose a dissertation topic, there was only one thing I could think of, only one story I wanted to hear and one topic I had sorely felt the absence of in studying the history of twentieth-century Britain: the history of me.

In my quest to understand the junction I stood at, the history of me was and is the history of the women I am of. The stories of the women who crossed half the world to reach a pitiful place, a pitiless place, but a place they survived nonetheless. In my research I ended up undertaking an oral history project with many first-wave Pakistani migrant women who had arrived to West Yorkshire between 1960 and 1980. Every one of them inspired me with deep fondness and love. I clung to their words and stories which came to me in a tongue I just about still understand but stumble over to speak. The process and the research meant so much to me because it fulfilled everything I wished academia would fulfil for me. It gave me my story, but also, it gave the women I so respect and love a chance to tell theirs and have it documented.

The history I learnt at home and the history I was taught institutionally have rarely coincided. Indian partition was touched on merely as an aside to post-war British politics in my degree; in my mind I envisioned the black-cloaked man who rode up to my grandmother's village and told them to 'Run, the Sikhs are coming' when formerly they had been friends and neighbours. This story stayed etched in my mind since my childhood days. I remember when my history teacher at school asked if anyone's parents or grandparents had fought in The Second World War. I put my hand up and explained how my great-grandfather, fighting for the British in the far-east against the Japanese, was taken as a prisoner of war in Malaysia. That was the first and last time the eastern front of World War Two and the Indian army were mentioned. Therefore, finding my own history and getting to address what had been so sorely absent from my white-washed curriculum was liberating. To read books whose authors had brown and female-coded names was rejuvenating. To hear theorisation of the South Asian female-migrant's gendering and racialization was dizzying. It was affirming.

And that is my problem when it comes to the academy. I can't deny that I have learnt and been equipped with much, but the knowledge I have craved has been lacking. Some jump in at this point to tell me then that I should carve out my own space—an institution is surely shaped by those who contribute to it. If by carving out that space I could help to change it, help recover knowledge that new generations could be taught; if I could do that perhaps it would be worthwhile. But I hesitate. I question how significant the recovery of excluded histories could be in an institution which has already placed boundaries and definitions on what is and isn't 'knowledge'. What impact could I have beyond becoming the tokenistic proof of a diversifying curriculum?

The vision I and those who rally behind the cry of 'decolonising our curriculums' share is about so much more than adding a handful of "harder-to-pronounce" names to our reading lists. It is about more than recovering 'non-European' resources and writings which are 'as worthy' as what is already read. A decolonised curriculum has to be about decolonising. Full-stop. To me that means not only contextualising the past, but also the present. That means studying European histories in the context of world history, studying the industrial revolution in the context of chattel slavery, and studying thinkers like Immanuel Kant in the context of colonialism. It also means recognising that what counts as and is defined as 'history' is determined entirely by present preoccupations rather than 'the past'. For example, the desire to presently manage the boundaries of who counts within the British nation shapes definitions of who and what past events count as "British History". Thus 'decolonising', if we are to consider it as a serious ideological urge, must be about not only diversifying sources but divesting from histories and forms of knowing which benefit the current hierarchical order of power.

Such work aimed at increasing the intellectual integrity of curriculums and disciplines like History has to also take into account the colonial nature of the institutions they are taught in – such as Cambridge. It has to take into account that the walls and halls here are not only physically and economically built and maintained on the back of empire and slavery/slave owning, but that they were intellectually built on it too. That the growth of the modes of thinking we so cherish are those intertwined with, born from and produced by colonialism and racism. That 'modernity' and 'the enlightenment' are just one possible narration of historical moments and processes that could and should just as legitimately be narrated as 'colonisation' and 'genocidal thinking'. Moreover, present day investments in fossil fuel industries and transnational arms corporations remind us that universities like Cambridge are also currently involved in exploitative neo-colonial projects, making 'decolonising' a very urgent and relevant project.

So where do we begin when our entire foundation of thought is unequal? What do we do when knowledge of Europe is essential to understanding the world, but one can study Europe and European thought without even a footnoted reference to elsewhere? The fact remains that the modules I studied on 'The History of the World' and 'History of Political Thought' centred on Europe, some European men, and European relationships. The implication from this is that 'The World' and 'political thought' do not exist without Europe. Outside of Europe there are only specificities – 'African philosophy', 'Oriental theology', 'South Asian modernity' – whereas in Europe you have absolutes and universals.

Amidst writing my third-year dissertation on Pakistani migrant women's experiences I would find my mind wandering to these questions. In this wider context of epistemic violence, validating their knowledges and experiences felt almost impossible because it demanded theorising, corroborating and testing them. At some level this meant being encouraged to abstract the people behind the stories, ridding them of their humanity. But was there not some value in telling the stories of these women in the institution anyway? Was it completely worthless to document them here? How could they gain legitimacy if not in the language already in place for that? And if that was so, why did legitimacy have to come from their marginalisation and dehumanisation? I resigned to being unsure. but I did not resign completely.

Whilst I remained in the institution I felt it was my duty to contribute to what little surface-scratches of change I could. Being a 'nuisance', being 'disruptive' and making people 'uncomfortable' were things I could do. Asking how my reading lists were comprised, raising alternative narratives in supervisions, demanding my oral history project be deemed as legitimate as any other source-base and creating alternative learning spaces where resources and knowledge were shared were all ways I did this. Sometimes, even just being present was disruptive enough.

Throughout this searching and learning and thinking I did about myself, about the institution, and about women, I came to realise that my perception of oppression, and, thus, my perception of liberation, was not one that many people were willing to accept. The more I took action to be a nuisance - intellectual and otherwise - and the more I wrote and shared what I wrote, I realised that what I was actually saying wasn't commonsensical to all around me. I realised that outside of FLY there were few at Cambridge who would subscribe to my same views. Few who would understand the need for my 'radicalism'. This was often most apparent in my feminism.

Declaring myself a feminist as a brown and Muslim woman threw up numerous questions and controversies for others. When I called myself a feminist, I was looking at a specific form of feminism and a specific notion of liberation which is inherent in my submission to Allah (Islam). To me, Islam makes resistance to oppression of every kind incumbent upon a worshipper. In that sense it is the most holistic approach to liberation I am aware of. Its potential is a vision of fundamental justice beginning with the prioritisation of emancipation from all forms of oppression. It is a vision which perceives no hierarchies of humankind based on cultural or social constructs; simply a vision of justice. Whether others agree or not, my own understanding of the Quran, shari'ah and the sunnah, and my ongoing learning about fiqh (interpretation), and the works of previous scholars, lead me to this conclusion. On this basis then, Islam is innately feminist in that worshipping Allah entails the pursuit of justice and liberation including, obviously, freedom from gendered oppressions. And this is what I view feminism to be.

Therefore, to my mind, feminists searching for 'equality' with men have inherently limited politics. They ignore the fact that not all women are equal to start with. There are inequalities amongst women which must be acknowledged before assuming to aim for 'equality' with men. Moreover, not all men are equal. If I fought to be equal to brown and Muslim men I would hardly have become freed from oppression but instead enter alternative gendered, racist and Islamophobic marginalisation and oppression.

Rather than 'equality' then, 'liberation' of all people from all oppressions is what drives my feminist logics. It can't be about being 'equal' to men (who face constricting gender-based ideas themselves) because to me, the situation that even the most privileged white man is in, is not one of liberation – it is one which rests on keeping others in subjugation. I do not want to be 'equal' in such a system. I do not want to see some women advancing at the expense of others. Rather than equal access to an oppressive apparatus, I demand the disruption of its norms and workings.

Feminism which seeks 'liberation' is more in tune with my vision of the world then. Liberation of all people from gender-based oppressions, racist oppressions, economic oppression, etc etc, all across the world – is the only way that I perceive true justice to come about. But who defines that liberation? In this definition, much like 'equality', lies another tussle I have had with mainstream feminism.

As a Muslim woman my liberation is often defined for me by others who judge my religion to be the central and sole barrier to my freedom. There are obviously deeply imperialist undertones to this idea of liberation which suggests one is 'free' when they fit Western, European and white standards of liberation – once they are free from their 'Otherness' (which at the same time you cannot rid yourself of). Under colonial domination we know that hypocrites like Winston Churchill, who opposed women's suffrage in the UK advocated imperial domination and exploitation in the name of 'saving' foreign women from 'uncivilised' and 'barbaric' men abroad. That same hypocritical narrative of saviourism which is actually about geopolitical goals is present in today's thinking about Muslim women's liberation too (see rhetoric around the invasion of Afghanistan in 2001 and burkini-ban in southern France 2016).[94]

I am told I cannot be liberated if I choose to cover my hair because Western ideas of liberation impose a particular view of the body (the context of Islamophobia enmeshed with The War On Terror[95] which suffuses our media and the ways we think of Muslim women as solely objects upon which the war for cultural hegemony is played out, is relevant in this). I am told I cannot be liberated if I choose not to be sexually active because this is deemed a 'backwards' attitude rather than a choice I have made myself. In this way then 'liberation' for Muslim women is essentially projected as becoming sexually available to a white male gaze. We are viewed as 'oppressed' if we deny that gaze our sexuality and our bodies.

This conceptualisation of 'liberation' is not for me. This conceptualis-ation of liberation is oppressive, suffocating and imperialistic. It forces Muslim women's 'assimilation' (rejection of Islam, or traits and behaviours associated with it) as the only possibility for freedom – a freedom which doesn't benefit Muslim women but aims to manage the boundaries of the nation by attempting to control which types of women reproduce cultural norms and thus which values remain hegemonic. Conceptions of liberation must be more radical than this.

My feminism therefore aims to challenge all supposed norms before being able to articulate itself fully. It aims to question all conceptions of equality, liberation, freedom, happiness, beauty, logic, power and

---

[94] Lila Abu-Lughod, Do Muslim Women Need Saving? 2013; and Fatima El-Tayeb, "Secular Submissions: Muslim Europeans, Female Bodies, and Performative Politics" in European Others: Queering Ethnicity in Postnational Europe, University of Minnesota Press, 2011.
[95] The term now used to refer to an international military and non-military assault led by the USA and European countries against the ambiguous and ever-present yet difficult to 'find', 'terrorists'.

truth because I know all of these concepts to be taught to us within a paradigm that allows oppression to continue and that maintains the status quo. My feminism is one which is simultaneously universal and individual. Which fights on all fronts but may also sometimes fight on seemingly-opposing fronts because oppression manifests itself in different ways in different contexts. A feminism which fights against rape being used as a weapon of war, but also fights for a world wherein we do not war. A feminism which fights against the sexualisation of female bodies, but also for greater space for female sexuality. A feminism for all people, but a flexible and active feminism. A critical feminism.

I have reservations then when I see 'this is what a feminist looks like' t-shirts being sold in mainstream high street stores; or bell hooks' quote 'feminism is for everybody' being made into mainstream graphics. Not because I do not want everybody to be a feminist; but because I know that not 'everybody's feminism' is for me, or will include me. That if everybody can call themselves A Feminist then feminism has likely become co-opted by capitalism or imperialism - it is likely too palatable, too diluted and too acceptable. I want everybody to be a feminist, but I want everybody to consider what that means beyond simply proclaiming it - does their conception also include everybody? For me, feminism has to be unacceptable. It has to offend. It has to be radical and possibly contradictory. If it is not these things then it is not working against the norms and structures that are so oppressive to so many. Instead, it is probably, once more, being manipulated into working within the structures; into claiming 'freedom' and 'equality' in acceptable ways, ways that only rearticulate or change but do not end oppression. Well, as someone whose existence is already unacceptable to society, that does not feel good enough.

Intersectional, radical, unpalatable and in the name of worshipping Allah; that is the feminism I'm about.

PART SEVEN:
Breaking the Silence of Oppression

whomever said the pen is mightier than the sword
has never had a gun to their head.

-

it is easy to be loud when you live in a house of mirrors –
cracked glass ceilings reveal an industrial complex
too complex for anyone to rebuild. you are

screaming sisterhood from the top of your lungs
and stepping on the necks of those whose speech
has never seen the light of day. step

back, this is not your time, these are not your
words to claim, and this is not your space
to inhabit, free of burden.

-Jun Pang

Borderless Activism and Solidarity with the Black Lives Matter Movement

Waithera Sebatindira

I'm getting tired of learning new names. Names I shouldn't know because no one would choose a viral hashtag over living, breathing anonymity. I'm tired of talking about the bodies to which those names now belong. And of watching eyes roll when I bring up each new victim, as if I enjoy dwelling on their murders. But mostly I'm getting tired of being tired, knowing there's no promise of rest ahead. Only more names to learn.

And I'm not alone in this. From around 2015 onwards I've observed growing solidarity for the Black Lives Matter movement in the US. Not only among my friends who are people of colour, but among our white peers as well. The success of a solidarity campaign I co-organised on campus for Michael Brown's family while facilitator for FLY is strong evidence of this. Over 200 people turned up to have their photos taken holding messages declaring that black lives matter and offering support to the university's black community. Similar solidarity campaigns were held at other universities across the UK as well, ranging from candlelit vigils to marches.

However, what's less encouraging is the fact that solidarity is about as far as a lot of people go. There's a feeling that some distance themselves from what's happening now in the US. An unspoken but firm belief that racism "isn't as bad" in the UK and so there's no need to evaluate what the murders of black Americans means for black lives everywhere else.

It's true that police brutality (while not a non-issue) is less prevalent here than in the United States. And, wholly aware that this is most likely down to my own class privilege, I don't fear state violence in England to the same extent that I fear it for family members that live in the US. Indeed, I often feel like I'm co-opting someone else's struggle when I use violence against African-Americans to prove a point about racism in the UK and elsewhere.

Yet it's illogical to think this way. Cultures and experiences of black people across the world do differ wildly from each other, but white supremacy is a global issue. The details of its exact manifestations change from region to region, country to country, even from one social class to another. But its ultimate aim remains the same. And if black lives have been devalued in the US to the point where they can be taken with such frequency – such violence – that is of relevance for black people everywhere.

There are probably a number of reasons why this can be difficult to see in Britain and, as a foreigner here going only from my own observations, there are a number I will miss. But one of them, I think, is the extent to which its racist past (and neo-colonial present) has been erased in dominant cultural discourse. This is most clearly evidenced by the rise in anti-immigration rhetoric here, which fails to acknowledge the role that Britain has played in destabilising the regions from which refugees are fleeing. Moreover, in virtually all mainstream discussions of Britain's role in the trans-Atlantic slave trade, it is portrayed solely as liberator. Not once in five years of secondary school education in this country did I learn anything about atrocities committed by the Brits across the Commonwealth. The almost total erasure in the mainstream of Britain's historical subjugation of people of colour therefore makes it extremely difficult to critically engage with racism here and have people see it as a real issue.

But this is changing. Britain is increasingly being forced to come to terms with its violent past. A 2015 documentary titled "Britain's

Forgotten Slave Owners"[96] aired on national television more honestly detailed the country's role in the slave trade and brought many necessary truths to light. Moreover, the hypocrisy of current anti-immigration hyperbole is increasingly being pointed out by some in mainstream media. So much still feels futile, especially given the political climate in England, and what's likely needed in addition is analysis that points to how the past is informing the present. But hope has to precede progress, and the examples above are two of many sources of hope.

In terms specifically of police violence, there are potential signs of North American influence. The story of Sheku Bayoh, a Sierra Leonean man who died in police custody in Scotland in May 2015, has gained a lot of traction in England. This is particularly heartening in light of the 509 Black and Asian deaths in police custody over the last 24 years, resulting in no successful prosecutions of officials involved. Rarely do these deaths make news, and I'm hopeful that this will change over time. Moreover, (while occupying the role of Home Secretary) Theresa May was specifically questioned on whether she believes black lives matter in the context of her review of deaths in custody. So there is evidence that, at the very least, the language of the US movement is beginning to be adopted in Britain.

And I remain hopeful that this will continue. Especially in light of the success of other international black movements in Britain. For example, the 'Rhodes Must Fall' campaign[97], which calls for the decolonisation of educational institutions, originated at the University of Cape Town in South Africa and has been adopted by students at Oxford University and inspired a similar movement at Cambridge as well. This is in addition to other independent movements at

---

[96] *Britain's Forgotten Slave Owners*, (2015). [TV programme] Two: BBC.
[97] 'Rhodes Must Fall' is a protest movement originating at the University of Cape Town. Students called for a prominent statue on campus of violent colonialist Cecil Rhodes to be removed, as well as for wider decolonial reforms across the University. This campaign sharply divided public opinion in South Africa and, after gaining global interest, sparked similar movements at universities across the world.

universities across the country which question Eurocentric curricula. That being said, it should be noted that such strong identification with a movement abroad is likely down to the fact that Eurocentric teaching practices are a widespread problem with which many people from a variety of nationalities can identify. Ultimately, the extent of police violence inflicted on black Americans is partially due to unique aspects of US culture than don't feature across the pond. But there is clear evidence, at least among black activists at university, that we understand that we're fighting a common enemy.

A wider understanding of this will build solidarity, as black British activists and black activists everywhere can see what they can contribute to the movement in the U.S., and vice versa. If racism is borderless, so, too, should be our activism.

(Insert Assault on Black Lives) (Insert Year)

"You rape our women and you're taking over our country"
I read these words and my palms become dirty and calloused
from the hands of those who tried to hold fast to red dirt
in our mother countries, clawing to hold on to dreams and lives
that can now be found at the bottom of the Atlantic
What to the Negro is the Fourth of July?
We have been standing on foreign soil
That we have tried for years to mix with red dirt palm prints
Yet all it has done is swirl and swirl and swirl.

And if Alice was right and land belongs to those
who have buried bodies in it
Then this indeed is our home too–even more
because it was built on our backs and the sweat from our brows
One life–millions of lives, for a country we aren't allowed to call home

"You rape our women and you're taking over our country"
I read these words and my womb contracts and bleeds
with the inherited memory of the 'massa's touch'
on young flesh as beautiful black bodies
are made ugly by the touch of power and lust for the 'exotic'.

You took her body and made it your own and
I AM HER DAUGHTER

Her legacy
Her pride and joy, who still is branded second-class by 'feminism'
Rejected in sisterhood and made monsters in bikinis by age 14
We have carried the lifeblood of our murderers and our rapists
With just one life to live, it has never been our own.

I was raised in a house of prayer
We join hands and ask God that where two or three
are gathered, He will answer our prayers
But I don't know what to pray for
When those invited into spaces of worship
Reign blood baths down on bowed heads and bent knees
And I think of little girls in white dresses in Birmingham streets.

Where are we safe?
I am murdered in streets
In churches
On front porches
In my own house
While holding candy
While just trying to breathe
Where can blackness survive?
And when can it not just survive, but thrive, and be *free?*

I lay my body down to try and claim the spaces
that I am not allowed to inhabit
And I am walked over
trampled to the margins
I walk into a room
and you feel uncomfortable
I speak my truth and you silence my life
I am weary
The unwanted becomes the annihilated.

Black is strength. Black is love. Black is beauty. Black is spiritual. Black is
power. Black is aware. Black is…
As my mantra gets longer, so does the time it takes to convince myself that
anyone is listening.
Some days I don't know if I've really survived
My heart barely feels like it's beating

-Odelia Younge

Who Do We Mourn?

Lola Olufemi

When devastating things happen, our instinct is to present a unified response. This is what makes us 'human.' We temporarily forget our differences and band together to help one another. This is what we saw when our news feeds were flooded with tributes, thoughts and kind messages to those suffering after the bomb blast that killed 130 people and injured many more in Saint Denis, Paris in 2015. This is what we saw in the countless people who temporarily changed their Facebook profile pictures in solidarity. Those small gestures were the ways people said: "I'm thinking about the victims."

Judith Butler puts it well when she says: "The question that preoccupies me in the light of recent global violence is, who counts as human? Whose lives count as lives? And, finally, what makes for a grievable life?"[98] What struck me about the response to the attacks was how much easier it was for people to share their condolences, their thoughts, anger and messages of hope for people who looked like them. The response clearly demonstrates that in the face of global violence, lives are not viewed in the same way. If we compare the disproportionate attention given to terrorist attacks in Western countries versus attacks as a result of Western intervention in the Global South, we are confronted with the idea that it is easier to grieve for those in the West because their lives are actualised by a deeply unequal power structure. They are people with families and histories whilst western hegemony frames the lives of those in the Global South

---

[98] Judith Butler, *Precarious Life*, New York: Verso, 2004

as collateral damage.

The selective and performative grief that is demanded online in the aftermath of terrorist attacks can be alienating for students of colour who are looking for spaces to process what has happened. In the construction of 'solidarity', every change of a profile picture, every tweet, every controversial status, feels like a reminder that in the face of tragedy, we forget to think critically. When we forget to think critically, we enable terrorist attacks to be mobilised by the media and the state to justify the intensification of surveillance and violence against marginalised groups.

It is possible to express sorrow and mourn the dead respectfully whilst also remaining aware of the fact that France is one of the largest exporters of Islamophobic propaganda. This means that the backlash from the Paris attacks will disproportionality affect Muslim people. I had friends whose first reaction was to check that their visibly Muslim friends and family in France were safe, because when Hollande stated that France's response would be "ruthless", it is clear that he was not thinking about the racialised bodies that would be discarded in his country's retaliation in the same way he was thinking about white French victims.

This same idea is echoed in the strange demands for Muslims to "condemn" the attacks. Muslims around the world owe us nothing. Not their apologies, not the signs that they will hold up to tell us these attacks were 'not in their name.' It is truly a sign that we treat Muslim people as a homogenous mass devoid of agency when we publicly hold them accountable for attacks that are as alien to them as to non-Muslims. Our insistence on reducing complex geopolitical situations to essentialist root causes reveals the ugliness in our responses to grief. It demonstrates that any assumption of 'shared humanness' is false because the second the West becomes the victim of violence, it repels non-white bodies and sends them into exile. They are forced to apologise, to console and with every demand we make of them in the face of terror, we normalise their dehumanisation.

Everywhere is in chaos, but the bubble that we exist in, one that is exaggerated even more by how insular Cambridge is, only ever bursts when white bodies become the victims of violence. It is then that we raise our heads, that the Senior Tutors send around emails, that we observe minutes of silence because we have learnt how to grieve for white people. We have yet to understand what it means to look outside of the West, outside of whiteness and extend that same compassion to the Global South, or indeed to members of the Diaspora who die at the hands of the state. Until we do, the same cycle continues – terror, grief, solidarity. Somehow students of colour find themselves constantly on the outside looking in.

How to Get to the Other End of a Dark Tunnel
Odelia Younge

While I was at Cambridge, I sometimes thought about staying in Europe. But Europe does not understand my particular pain.

I stayed up late one night while working on my master's thesis to listen to the grand jury decision on whether or not to indict Darren Wilson for the murder of Michael Brown. I was writing the beginning of my conclusion when the live newsfeed began rolling across my screen. I knew as I listened to the man's words that this would end like every other time. Each claim of media blame and 'unfounded' statements and social media frenzy drove knives through my chest as I felt my world sink a little deeper into the numbness that comes from familiar pain.

I read a post online from my friend Tabias that said, "Everyone's guilty except the people who are." Those words are bitterly true. I shut the feed off a few minutes past the declaration that Wilson would not be indicted, and felt the first few angry tears sting my eyes and blur my vision. I could no longer clearly see the conclusion to my paper. I hadn't been able to see the conclusion for days.

In one of my supervisions[99] my supervisor asked me if my master's thesis would engage with theories of a post-racial America. I felt a bubble of laughter swell in my chest at the thought of such a

---

[99] Supervisions are teaching sessions for a student (or small group) led by a specialist in the subject being studied. At the master's level, supervisions are led by the master's student supervisor who is assigned to them to help guide their studies.

suggestion. But I quelled the feeling. I came to Cambridge because I wanted to learn more, and I thought, at the time, that I wanted to find a way to get a seat at the table that is allowed to produce knowledge. But on most days I simply felt lost.

In my term paper on the positive impact Afrocentric education for black children, I argued that it would give them a different way of conceptualizing the world, one in which they would not have to be assessed through a lens already bent on destroying them and telling them that 'different is deficient.' For them, self-knowledge would be the highest form of knowledge, and educational spaces would be redefined and would not sell black children the idea of socio-economic mobility and safety, but rather the tools to become their own producers of knowledge – of themselves, of their people, and of the world. And I longed for that world myself.

That paper led me to my thesis work. I came across works on critical youth studies, and I wondered about how we as children came to actualize the world we produced for ourselves in our own lives. I developed a concept for my master's thesis around looking into how black youth - black male youth - came into their own identities. I had always been interested in positioning theory, which outlines how in any conversation or interaction, we assume a position.[100] But what happens when someone else believes they have a right to position us? Even in re-positioning ourselves from that external placement, others feel they have a societal right to maintain how they have placed us. There are three options here: 1) become catatonic, unable to do anything in life because of the feeling of not having agency, 2) pursuit of negative actions because of the feeling of not having agency, or 3) finding creative means to assemble a new position, outside the dominant paradigm.

The third option is where my work landed. My questions led to my development of the theory of *heterotopic spaces of internal resistance*

---

[100] Harré, Rom. *Positioning Theory: Moral Contexts of Intentional Action*, Oxford: Blackwell, 2003.

(HSIR), a theory of identity representation in marginalised youth. HSIR are the real and imagined spaces created as sites of resistance to the dominant discourse, in order to engage with alternative identities. My thesis centered on the lives of eight young black men and who they chose to be in the face of a world that tried to write a story for them. I saw in them that a critical nature of the work of forging one's identity for oneself was the recognition of the nuances of blackness. Once we see the work another would have also had to do to get to these identities, revolutionary paths become more clear because we can better honor the collective work against anti-blackness.

But I had not finished the conclusion to my thesis. I couldn't seem to bring myself to write the summary of this work, nor did I feel encouraged to do so. The only thought in my head was to rip up each page of the paper because it *did not matter*. I was not sure what I thought I would find here at Cambridge. I was not sure how exactly to fit into what felt like a fixed narrative for black bodies within white spaces.

That night, after hearing the grand jury decision, I fell asleep with tear stained cheeks. I clung a little tighter to James Orbinski's words that if we can imagine a better tomorrow, then it can come to pass[101] and to Robin D. G. Kelley's assertion that we can and must envision the end of oppression.[102] My grip was so tight on those words some nights that I could feel them squeezing through the creases of my fingertips. I was selfishly grateful that night to not have four classes to teach the next morning. To not have to smile through curriculum that itself often felt like it did not matter. Because there are days when I am too weak to smile and say that things will be different one day. Days when I cannot mouth the hollow words that we should be grateful to be 'free' and alive in the 21st century.

---

[101] Orbinski, James. *An Imperfect Offering: Humanitarian Action for the 21st Century*. Toronto: Doubleday Canada, 2008.
[102] Kelley, Robin D. G. *Freedom Dreams: the Black Radical Imagination*. Boston :Beacon Press, 2002.

I am grateful for sunrises that have become precious for so many of my people, and the chance to try to begin again. I will not forget their names. I cannot forget their names. And I think about how the work is not done. We must keep going. We don't all get a tomorrow to try again to find conclusions. Being unapologetically black is too often a privilege.

It has been summer after summer of burning. I matriculated into Cambridge on the heels of the summer of 2014: a summer of Ferguson riots after Michael's body was left in the streets and Eric's breath was stopped. As we later witnessed Tamir killed for daring to be a child with an imagination, Sandra murdered, and Baltimore's fiery uprising when Freddie was left to die. Many of us found that what we had been experiencing was that none of us could breathe.

During matriculation, I signed a large book filled with centuries of names of those who walked the hallowed halls of privilege before me. I sat and dined in an extravagant hall where faces like mine aren't readily represented in the multitude of paintings that line the walls.[103] I sometimes think about my name floating inside that pristine matriculation book, void of the markers of race, but *I cannot keep calm because next could always be me.*

I have been filled with tears and raging anger that bubbles up at times and threatens to swallow me whole. Over the years, I have witnessed many loved ones come undone by the news headlines and the carefully planned stripping away of black bodies, black presence, and black voice. They silence those who say what they don't want to hear because dead people certainly don't tell their own stories.

I have inherited most of the calm, contemplative strength of my mother. I used to find myself in the midst of large groups of people and force myself to smile, because I felt like I should. I had decided I would rather be silent in those situations than branded an 'angry

---

[103] I am very grateful for the Black Cantabs project for unearthing the history of so many of Cambridge's black students of the past.

black woman'. White comfort often leads to black isolation, especially in institutions of power and elitism. But some labels are worn better and braver than others, and for far too long the badge of 'courage' we gave to those who could bear high levels of injustice in silence was just another way to make sure most of us remained complicit in our own destruction. I don't - I can't - do that anymore.

All of this while sitting in a university that is not constructed to provide tools to address this.

Monachopsis: the subtle but persistent feeling of being out of place

When I find myself in spaces that weren't created for me, as token and as invisible as those places beg me to be, I can't be erased. No, I was here. I signed the book, and I ate in those halls. I forged my own tools. I leave my mark in the ways that I find and know how. You can't forget something or someone that refuses to give you the power to do so, nor is willing to engage by those rules.

People often ask me why I research topics related to black boys and not black girls (as though there are no overlapping issues). The answer to that is long and complicated, but I have found that this work researches my life as well. Interviewing the eight young black men for my case study intensely reminded me of how early my own journey began to represent my own identity, and how that work proved necessary as I spent more time in spaces like Cambridge.

I have been encouraged in this journey by amazing mentors too. From my tutors and professors in undergraduate, to my supervisor at Cambridge, who always owned the things she could know while admitting to the things she did not, and giving me all the space I needed to go find that information. She was the supervisor I needed at Cambridge. She took a bright-eyed but cautious woman in October 2014 and helped her get to July without making compromises on her research. I remember one conversation we had after I had written an especially theoretically worded section of my second essay. She looked at me and talked about how sometimes when people find themselves in places like Cambridge, they are seduced into the rhetoric of the ivory towers that tell them writing must be a particular way. However, in reality, that writing only does the job of shutting others out of academia, and oftentimes those others are the ones who the research claimed to be for. She eloquently spoke to me about the type of research that can be done *with* the communities the research is about and not *about* or *to* them. She always ended our supervisions with the same declaration: to say a complex thing in the simplest, most accessible way was true elegant writing. I truly appreciated her.

Being mindful of changes that we can be susceptible to within powerful institutions becomes half of the battle in these spaces. At the AERA conference in Chicago that spring (2015), a black male academic reminded a room full of aspiring academics of colour that if you make compromises while trying to be a compassionate researcher working within communities and putting their trust and relationship with you as your top priority - you never stop making those compromises, and you harm those you wanted to help bring about healing to. Another academic told the story of how he took hip-hop out of his final dissertation because someone told him he needed to, and even though it won many prizes, he felt it would have been even better – and more him – with it in.

Being in academia as a black woman is not an act of resistance in itself. Being a black woman in academia who is there to make a statement that genius has many faces and mannerisms is revolutionary. In the journey to liberation, there needs to be liberatory practices within academia as well.

When I began editing my thesis, I told the people I asked to edit it that I would not compromise on the findings. I refused to cut the part of my work that came from the participants themselves. I had made a promise to them to tell their stories as honestly as I could, and I would keep that promise. In my master's thesis I wrote:

"That is what I have come to embrace in my life, which is why I recognised the beginnings of such a consciousness in my participants. This internal

resistance I began to put words to is a rejection of spaces solely defined by structural and cultural barriers. Instead, it is a space created entirely from their construction of reality and crafted as a space of transgression. It is a space to not address the 'one more thing' but to perceive the world and build more spaces that boldly state, "I am not here for you."

It is what FLY and the women of colour in it do. It's what I've seen so many black women in this world do.

How do you get to the other end of a dark tunnel with your head and your heart intact? The answer is you don't. At least not by yourself. I thank God each day for flows of survival in the form of family and friends at Cambridge, home, and abroad, who made me smile and laugh and dance. Those eight young men saved me. As they found ways to survive outside of a desire to forge identities in relation to the white dominant discourse, I was encouraged to continue finding my own. I didn't write my thesis about them, I wrote it for them and with them—their lives guiding the pen until the final words hit the pages.

Holy Water

They said come down to the water
You can bathe in the cool drops of the water
Water that washes away all the uncleanliness and sin

But there is a sin of being in these parts
Those who the call to join in the water
Was not a real invitation
Not a real welcoming
As black and brown bodies are stains
in the eyes of those who believe that
water only washes to whiteness

And black and brown bodies cannot be cleaned
They do not have the ability to be scrubbed clean
And when placed in the water, whiteness fears–
It fears the muddying of clear waters

Because if I, and my brothers and sisters
Were to dive inside the vastness of the water
We would float along on our backs
Watching as the water dispersed and rippled around us
Beautiful, bold, dark glimpses of hope
As we cut our way through its depth
And there would be something in the water–
The crystal clear, deep reminder
That blackness survives
No matter how hard you try to wash it away

-Odelia Younge

PART EIGHT
Reflections

On Being From

To be, or not to be; that is a question, but one perhaps, wrongly put. "To be" is easy; "to be" does not tie you down; "to be" is light, at least, lighter than "to be from" – I can be without being from somewhere I do not belong; I can be without thinking, without returning to roots I am not sure even exist, without looking at myself in the mirror and wanting to see something less incongruous to the setting. To have been from somewhere, to be from nowhere, to be setting off elsewhere, to be returning to a place where, logically, I must have left – to want to have a "from" and for "from" to always be just out of reasonable reach – to be, or not to be from; that is the question

-

That I may
That I may be near you, and see your sights again;
that I may cross this river and find my way back home;
that I may trace the distance between your land and mine
without a tremble in my fingers and without need
for a straight edge besides; that I may

know you again, and see you in a new light; that I may
return to the dust that once threatened to stop me
from breathing; that I may find the harbour for
the banks that threaten everyday to break loose;

that I may reach an end,
stop, and no longer be suspended

Halfway here and halfway there.
-
What is and what is to be is not your fault.

-Jun Pang

Reflections on Decolonising The Curriculum

Lola Olufemi

The extract below is the transcript of a speech given at Goldsmiths University in 2017 detailing the rationale behind the work done by a group of postcolonial students in the English Faculty who attempted to decolonise the curriculum and more importantly, the university. This campaign received widespread media attention.

"Literary texts circulate in society not just because of their intrinsic merit, but because they are part of other institutions such as the market or the education system. Via these institutions, they play a crucial role in constructing a cultural authority for the colonizers, both in the metropolis and in the colonies."[104]

For me, these words from Ania Loomba present the case for decolonising the curriculum. Because literature deals with the subjective, it is often cast as an apolitical field. We're told over and over again not to burden the text with subjectivity or analytic readings that highlight how gender and race come to shape our experiences of reading and writing. But here Loomba points out that literature has a purpose beyond pleasure, it cannot be separated from the structures that dictate our lives and structures that many in the field of English Literature are scared to claim. Literature is fundamental in the maintenance and reproduction of those structures, it is one of the driving forces behind 'the market' that shapes our education. What I learnt from studying literature at Cambridge is that the canon as we know it is central in the formation of a hierarchy of value and perhaps most crucially, the

---

[104] Loomba, Ania. *Colonialism/postcolonialism*, (London: Routledge), 2005.

creation of taste. That is how we get to a stage where there are texts we don't dare critique because they're understood, widely, to have intrinsic merit. That is what enables the creation of cultural authority which is signified by the "canon," and shapes the field in which we study. It is the reason that so often, writers and critics from the Global South, whose focus is the consequences of colonial rule – memories, contexts and impacts can be let off of curricula without a second thought.

It was being faced with readings that acknowledged power and its role in shaping history that prompted discussion amongst a group of third year English students about what a decolonised curriculum and more importantly, a liberated university might look like. Decolonisation is not just about curricula, it is about the marketised university's complicity in neocolonialism. It's about the arms trade, climate justice and recognising that our universities are not only sites of violence for students of colour but that they also enact violence across the world. When we demanded decolonisation, we were thinking about what we learn and how we learn, why we learn, the environments in which frameworks of knowledge come to be established. How what we learn adds to the language of justification for colonialism. By that I mean, how culture (which literature is part of) shapes political decisions – the decision to occupy another country or refuse to repatriate stolen land and artifacts. What does it mean to move through an entire English degree without ever being asked to engage critically with authors from the global south? What does it mean to be taught exclusively by white lecturers and supervisors? How does this maintain and reproduce cultural authority and how does that turn us, as recipients of this education, into individuals who are unable to grapple with colonial history and its wide reaching impacts. What does it mean to have Pope, Swift, Shakespeare and Dickens held up as exemplary, without a robust examination of the contexts in which these writers emerged? To examine how the industrial revolution was aided by colonial rule and how this is crucial in configurations of "outsiders," "the other," "the orient," that reoccur in the writing of someone like Joseph Conrad, for example. Or to speak of the "intrinsic merit" of certain writers without paying attention to how merit is itself subjective.

That is exactly what curricula does. It is an extension of the institution and demarcates which people, kinds of knowledge and ways of being are acceptable and which are not. This is why we consistently came up against criticisms from staff and students who maintained that nothing of merit had emerged from writers from the global south and that was the reason those authors were not studied. Or ironically, there was no one to teach those texts and they weren't relevant to questions of form, genre and so on.

Here we must also consider how a curriculum that purposefully silences dissenting voices, especially those from the colonies, is doing the job that the discipline was created to do. English Literature, when introduced under colonial rule, was about the maintenance of cultural authority from the coloniser to the colonised. Said speaks of how "Europe did command the world and the Imperial map licensed the cultural vision"[105] and, "In the first place, the history of fields like comparative literature, English studies, cultural analysis, anthropology can be seen as affiliated with the Empire and, in a manner of speaking, connecting Empire to Secular Interpretation." In many ways, the curriculum as we saw it, was training a class of people to occupy elite positions without giving us the critical capacity to question with what we were learning. Without undoing our attachment to cultural authority. We were being taught to maintain the status quo. When we began to challenge this, we saw the pushback because we had been deemed as going too far. We were overstepping what was expected of us as students: that we moved through the institution without ever asking questions or speaking back to the canon. I think this was exemplified in the ways that the students who spoke up and out were problematised, in the faculty, in the media, all with the intention of silencing.

---

[105] Said, Edward W. Culture and Imperialism. (New York: Knopf) 1994.

So then, what did decolonisation mean to us? Decolonisation is as Fanon argues, a process of complete disorder. It is not a defined set of practices but instead seeks, amongst other things, to reassign cultural authority from the global north. It is about the repatriation of land and resources, it is about dismantling the racism that enables colonialism and neo-colonialism to continue to this day. It is the complete dismantling of the concept of the nation state. It is about discovering lost languages, histories and a reimagination of the self without the violence of the colonisers gaze. It is about equity. It is many things. But within an institution, that process of disorder becomes even more unclear. Short of tearing the institution to the ground and rebuilding it, what can be done? Reforms. Changes, which are a worthwhile endeavour and I think, provide the framework for imagining a liberated future. When we wrote the letter, we understood our location in an elite institution. Though our demands may have seemed piece-meal, our positionality enabled us to open up a wider conversation about what decolonising the institution might look like, even if it was impossible. We became *saboteurs* as theorised by Fred Moten in *The Undercommons*.[106]

What we gathered is that decolonisation is not a metaphor for the way we would like our society to change and I take this idea from Eve Tuck and K. Wayne Yang[107] who express discomfort at the way decolonisation is so quickly subsumed by institutions as to strip it of its meaning and take the focus away from undoing settler colonialism. But cultural significance and value are a key part of colonial rule –so what we did was to begin to unpick them from where we were. We began with pushing for greater investment in the postcolonial department; placing texts in conversation with each other in a critical manner, hiring more specialists in the literature of the Global South, questioning pre-established hierarchies of value within the discipline, reforming teaching styles and most crucially, eroding the barriers

[106] Harney, Stefano and Fred Moten, *The Undercommons: Fugitive Planning & Black Study*, 2013, Print.

[107] Tuck, Eve & Wayne Yang, K, *Decolonization Is Not a Metaphor. Decolonization*. 1. (2012).

between disciplines. We cannot talk about English Literature without sociology, history, philosophy, it makes no sense to demarcate the bounds of "the literary" as distinct and separate from those other fields. We did this with the hope of building a critical consciousness that aided the other processes that are crucial to this project. We did it with a seriousness and a purpose, as students who understood that when we begin to challenge the designated thought leaders of any discipline, we clear the road for voices that have been purposefully suppressed. For us, English Literature was about that: voice. Who gets to speak and why? Whose narrative takes centre stage?

We didn't have all the answers but we prepared ourselves to engage in a conversation that has played out and will continue to play out long after those who began it have left the institution. We left behind a memory of the work we we did, working groups, renewed energy. We breathed live into the conversation whilst we were there. The task now is to make sure that it remains on the agenda and disrupt the faculty's attempts to carry on as if it were business as usual. It is not.

Defining Myself for Myself

Suhaiymah Manzoor-Khan

One September afternoon before beginning my final year at
Cambridge I found myself in the familiar living room of my grandparent's home. It is a room where I still hear echoes of my childhood
laughter and can almost see every reel of camcorder tape ever filmed
there playing one on top of the other. But it is also a room which has
become full of realisations with age. A room bearing witness to words
and memories whose hurt or sad depths I have only discovered with
hindsight. Today was one of those days. My grandparents were
retracing memories with me, guiding my fingertips over places, people
and moments of the past. I found it impossible to ignore how our
fingers bumped into and over ridges and scars revealing the way
colonialism continued to haunt our family. The way the pain of leave
home had not purged it but only grotesquely refigured it.

As my grandmother later checked how my nose piercing was healing
she recalled, amusedly, how white women had ridiculed her for her
nose rings when she first came to England. How they had mocked her
mendhi,[108] the fact she had six children so young, and that she did not
wear a wedding band. She quipped, 'I told them I had married a man,
not a ring!' then chuckled. She chuckled at the way everybody wants
their nose pierced now and people clamour for mendhi. In that
moment, in her light-heartedness and ability to snap from past to
present, I painfully realised the simultaneous hurt of holding onto

---

[108] Mendhi is a form of body art in which decorative designs are created on a person's body
using paste made from the powdered dry leaves of the henna plant.

your 'othered' cultural norms and facing violence for it, and the pain of those norms later being abstracted from you and celebrated in spite of your dehumanisation. I felt the aching that women so often bear as the carriers of the traits and behaviours called 'culture' and saw the physicality of imperialist white supremacy and her bravery and poise in the face of it.

A few months later, back at University, this moment often rose to my mind. I thought about it when a white woman in my college persisted to deride my critique of her treatment of myself and others with South Asian heritage, whilst also consistently enjoying wearing pretty ornaments like bindis and saris. I thought about how this exemplified the violence in the contradiction of the white women who mocked my grandmother fifty-five years ago, and white women now wanting to look as she did without having to pay the price of being a brown immigrant woman. That is the price of existing in a context and history of racism and colonialism and being shunned, shamed and stigmatised, deemed uncouth, ugly and unwelcome, for wearing the same things white women now celebrate.

That same moment and others like it were what made a degree in History so important to me. History wasn't just about learning others' stories, but about telling and contextualising my own. I knew, from places like my grandparents' living room, that there were unarticulated hurts and unknown injustices as well as untold stories of triumph to be told. Sometimes they came to my mind when I was hunched over my laptop in the University Library. The juxtaposition of those memories with my location kept me grounded and motivated to make sure the history lessons that came in the form of anecdotes and offhand comments from my grandparents, were known outside of their living room.

This was what sparked my original oral-history project and dissertation on first-wave Pakistani migrant women to West Yorkshire in the first place. When I had completed it, I remember holding the bound copy in my hands and being surprised about how small it seemed compared to how large it felt. I considered what the point of all the interviews and hard work had been and why it had mattered to document old immigrant women's lives in this way.

I knew these women existed and they knew they existed. But the institutions, academia and books I had spent my degree interacting with didn't seem to know they existed or had stories of their own. By overlooking their existence, they did an injustice to mine too. And whilst it was one of the most privileged forms of feeling subversive that there can be; and whilst academic validation is not necessary for one to exist — writing out those stories, articulating those realities and printing them out felt a worthwhile, if small, contribution during my time at Cambridge. I hoped, in some way, that that little bundle of paper could stand in defiance of a remarkable silence when it came to Pakistani immigrant women's lives - erased in both migration history, and so-called 'women's history'. And I hoped it could be a testament to the fact I had existed in that space. I hoped that sitting on the shelves of the history faculty library it would represent a corner of my grandparent's living room in a place it was never supposed to be known.

Alongside representation for my grandparents, that living room, and my history, was a desire to define myself, too. To be the author of my own story which had, for too long, had voyeuristic authors. Definition through authorship became ever-more important to me as I realised that writing was a way not only to express and give meaning to things, but a way to imagine them anew.

Imagining through writing is necessary because there are not always frames of reference for the ways I, as a grandchild of immigrants, am existing. The society and culture that is 'mine' is constantly new and being produced. There are no real conventions, and this often means life is either a task of shrinking to the frameworks of others or creating my own. More likely it is the latter. Creating anew is a necessity because I am in new situations and predicaments for which there are not always old or familiar routes or words which make sense. This is not to be 'hybrid' or have 'one foot in either culture' because that fails to account for the complexity, historicity, and malleability of 'culture' in the first place, and of what is really being done in the second place: something entirely new.

I have only slowly come to terms with this. Where my grandparents' history ends and my own begins is an impossible line to find. Sometimes I long for a simpler story of static cultural continuity. I watch Youtube clips of Hindi films, search out Punjabi songs on the internet and ache to feel in touch with a place I imagine myself to have come from. But I recognise deep down that I am watching clips of women dressed in clothes I don't wear, singing in a language I need subtitles to properly understand, and making references to norms that feel like a whispered memory more than anything I know to be substantially true. These things aren't 'mine', and more often than not, they are exaggerations, constructions, and romanticisms. Yet even whilst I recognise that and embrace the chance to live creatively and exist in new ways, I also feel a sadness. Sadness because those things might have meant something different to me had they not been unravelled and stripped from me in the process of my family's migration to Britain and attempted integration and assimilation for acceptance and survival. I resent never having been allowed a proper chance to hold onto some things that are a part of my story in a convoluted way.

Nonetheless, my story is ongoing. Throughout my time at Cambridge and learning to 'define myself for myself' in order to protect against the definitions others wanted to apply to me, I also began to uncover how dangerously close I had been to being 'crunched into other people's fantasies for me and eaten alive'.[109] This was not only in the straightforward sense that I was overwhelmed and mentally depleted by others' expectations and categorisations. At some stage I think I had also come to so resent those fantasies that I actually believed in them and flung them ontoothers. For as long as I believed

---

[109] Audre Lorde, 'Learning from the 60s', 1982 - full quote: "If I didn't define myself for myself, I would be crunched into other people's fantasies for me and eaten alive."

that the less 'Other' I was, the better I was, I myself was entrapped in and perpetuating those fantasies. It was a form of self-hatred that would have, if unacknowledged, eaten me alive in the end. Self-hatred can be rife in the most casual of ways when people are living and imagining themselves amidst and against other people's fantasies. One of my only school teachers of Pakistani heritage once told me and the rest of my Urdu class (also all of Pakistani heritage) not to apply to a certain sixth-form because it was 'full of apnay'. Apnay is a word which literally means 'people like us'. Her swallowed belief that brown was automatically worse, that 'we' were automatically worse, was no anomaly. It was the result of fantasies imposed on us through imperialist, Eurocentric and Islamophobic narratives which fill our lives. Therefore, in 'defining myself for myself' I have also made an active effort to love myself and extend that love to others like me. I have to love them, for to love them is to love me. And when I begin to define myself beyond the categories of others – beyond epistemologies rooted in colonial logics, beyond race, and gender, and culture and more in the sense of history, and context and circumstance – my definition of "those like me" becomes broader and more capable of being massively collaborative. When I say that defining myself has also been an effort to love myself and others like me, I am really saying I have tried to use tools other than 'the master's'.[110]

To love myself is to denaturalise the way the world is – to point out that being marginalised and oppressed and maligned are not just natural or normal circumstances but deliberate and contingent outcomes of violent historical processes. Therefore, to love myself is to call the master's tools what they are – colonialism rather than enlightenment, slavery rather than industrial revolution. It is to call the master's house what it is – a structure upholding colonial white supremacy.

To define and love myself in order to be capable of loving others, also requires I accept the love of others. There is an Islamic saying from

---

[110] Audre Lorde, 'The Master's Tools Will Never Dismantle The Master's House'.

from the Prophet Muhammad (SAW)[111] that one should 'love for your brother what you love for yourself'. The premise is that we love ourselves – and surely that also entails accepting others' love.[112]

However, in creating, representing, imagining and defining myself, my own history, and new paradigms, I have often made little space to be loved. Though love and solidarity with other people of colour — especially women and non-binary people of colour like those in FLY — has been an undeniable aid to me, it took me time to accept the aid of others. For a long time, this stemmed from my experience of people trying to fight my fight for me and in doing so assuming they knew better than me what my liberation looked like. It also stemmed from my experience of the white-saviorism Muslim women often face, and that when others talked about my liberation they were more likely to be listened to than I was - I was resentful. Perhaps I was supposed to be grateful, but often I was resentful. I feared being excluded from my own liberation.

It was a dogged version of me then, a scared and untrusting version, that was confronted with the words of a close white friend in the summer of 2015. She tried to voice how tragic it was to love me but be told to leave me to my own fight. I was taken aback. This struck me. I had been too wary and afraid to consider and acknowledge this might be the case for anyone. However, what 'helping me to fight' would look like had many meanings. Some of the most important things my close white friends have done has been showing their love through their listening and not their talking - their hurting with me, not consoling me. In many ways, learning to accept their love and allowing them to love a me who was continuing to define herself was an important step in terms of loving myself. It taught me also that love that is full of honesty has to be full of confrontations and contradictions. That it requires vulnerability that can be painful and jarring in the way it

---

[111] S.A.W. is an abbreviation of the Arabic phrase, salla-llahu-alayi-wa-sallam, a prayer to express gratitude for the Prophet and that Allah exalt him.
[112] Farid Esack, *On Being Muslim.*

destabilises easy binaries.

In the same way that extending my love to other people of colour and Muslims was to overcome the fantasies of others, accepting the love of people who weren't, was to trust that my definition could trump their fantasies. It was to have the faith and hope that they would love me as defined by myself, even when I wasn't present. That that love would be proactive and not passive – that it would hound them to stand up for justice even when against themselves, and push them to denaturalise their own 'houses', too.

Unlearning and learning, unbecoming and becoming, imagining and defining are all parts of the quiet revolution — the one that goes on inside oneself. This journey was always simultaneous to the educational, campaigning and collaborative political work I did at Cambridge. Therefore even if at first Cambridge was an experience of alienation, fear and dislocation, the lesson I left with was one of hope. Hope that the revolution does not only have to be internal but, in fact, that every interaction has revolutionary potential when it is actively loving and vulnerable. Hope that proactive love has a radical potential to shift and destabilise the hierarchies, oppressions and paradigms the world is built upon – because love can be nothing if not the active pursuit of every single being's liberation and recognition that that is bound up with oneself. Therefore to define and love oneself is to realise how absolutely dependent we are upon one another and that it is always better to risk our comfort, than someone else's safety.

I never expected that I would leave Cambridge with such a message, or with such bright hope when it stood for the structures and hierarchies I loathe, surrounded me with everything I am not, and perpetuated systems that oppress. Still, seeing and experiencing Cambridge first-hand instilled me with the passion I have today. It instilled me with the need and desire for justice and liberation. Through realising that the tools given to me to supposedly attain all goals in my life were ones those institutions themselves had crafted in a system founded on oppression and violence, bolstered my confidence. I could reject those tools and use my own.

It would be accurate to say that I was radicalised at Cambridge then. Being put through a pressure-cooker experience of institutional racism based in historical coloniality really gave me critical insight into how structures uphold themselves, but also how often our efforts to resist are so easily co-opted.

These realisations, along with meeting some of the most inspiring and excellent people I now know, led me to decide that maybe I could embrace the fear and uncertainty that often clouded my vision. Maybe I could turn it into hope and set out not only to alter and shift paradigms, but to live a new one. There is certainly anxiety and fear in this, but there is also liberation.

To exist in new ways is to defy other people's fantasies and aim to dismantle them too. It will always tickle me that this is the message I leave Cambridge with: the secret knowledge under my tongue. On my graduation day I held my degree certificate in my hand but in my heart I held the real lessons — those learnt outside the libraries and seminar-rooms. Many people's parents asked why I did not kneel before our College President in my graduation ceremony and if it was because I was religious. I simply told them that an act of deference to an institution that had so suffocated me made no sense and asked instead if they could think of a reason why I should kneel. None could.

As Assata Shakur famously said, 'The schools we go to are reflections of the society that created them. Nobody is going to give you the education you need to overthrow them. Nobody is going to teach you your true history, teach you your true heroes, if they know that that knowledge will help set you free.'[113]

On my graduation day the paper in my hand was meaningful because of the structures around me which made it so. But the people I met here, especially in FLY, the ideas they shared with me and the love they taught me were the most significant things I take away from that

---

[113] Assata Shakur, *Assata: An Autobiography.*

place. I have been inspired by every unacceptable person I know, by every identity which disrupts the certainty of my own, every life narrative which defies the time-bounded milestones we presume, every refusal of categorisation and every brave and revolutionary person I existed alongside. Without loving and being loved by them I would still be trapped by the fantasies of other people. Instead, the unlearning of the world has already begun to set me free.

A Year of Becoming

Odelia Younge

You do not have to be a fire
for
every mountain blocking you.
you could be a water
and
soft river your way to freedom
too.
–options[114]

Returning to the U.S. after my master's program ended was the first time that I did not begin a new journey with time spent reflecting in my childhood home, A Town Where Time Does Not Reside.[115] I boarded my flight in London and went straight to a new beginning in Philadelphia, the weight of time zones and memories jarring me in the journey.

Before I went back to the U.S. I took a trip to Greece to celebrate finishing my master's. There was a moment during my celebratory vacation that I was standing on a rocky hill by a lighthouse on the island of Mykonos with a breathtaking view of the sea in all its blue-green majesty. In that moment I closed my eyes and felt the weight

---

[114] waheed, nayirrah. *salt*, 2013.

[115] I refer to the town where I grew up, Belleville, Indiana, as A Town Where Time Does Not Reside as a nod to the feeling that time moves slowly in a small town. This has been an ongoing means of me talking about it since I started my blog Footprints in the Air, in 2011.

and wonder of the end of one journey and the beginning of another wash over me. And in that moment, I simultaneously wanted to cry, laugh, sigh and rejoice for everything that was and was about to be. As I let myself feel all of these emotions swirl in me at once, I thought of what it has meant for me to be a black woman living abroad, existing in these systems of power and elitism, and what it would mean to return home to America. Again.

The U.S. is not my homeland of birth, as I often explain to people. It is my homeland by the choice of my parents, as they believed it to be the place where their children—especially their daughters—would be able to realise the things that were true about themselves and bcome everything they wanted. Long ago too, however, my ancestors came across oceans. Some as indentured servants from India, some slaves from the Gold Coast of Africa, and others, still, the European explorers who first cast stones of 'inferior' towards the other parts of me. While I am all of those stories, I belong most to the land and the blackness of my people. And while much of my childhood was marked by those who wished to convince me I was the 'exception' of my people, if my time in the U.S. has shed light on one truth, it is that there are no exceptions when it comes to black people who assert their humanity through the means they themselves deem fit. While I could sit in a room and smile and make conversation with those who did not see this right of mine, I was all the while *dangerous*.

Is it love and admiration if they only love and admire you through a particular lens? Or only when you stay inside the boxes they created? The spaces that they have named? Though America is the site of some of my most painful memories, it is also the site of my greatest triumphs. While I was in many ways forged by its fires, and spat out with a new "birth certificate" in hand, I often felt anxious, as if surrounded by walls closing in. I wanted and needed to see what lay beyond this country, what different ways of being and currencies in life were sought and fought for on other lands. I think that's why I loved the red dirt of Ghana so much the year I lived there after my under-graduate studies. I felt centuries of feet clambering across the land,

and the strength of women carrying physical and emotional weights of home and family. My love of travel was born out of something I reflect on still: the ability to view my life from the outside looking in. It gives me clarity to see what it is that makes me unique and the spaces I am crafting in my life on a daily basis.

But we often romanticise leaving. We envy those with the wander-lust and means of taking a plane ride across oceans to countries many only dream of or read about. We imagine them escaping the racism and emotional and mental turmoil of being black in America, sitting in smoke-filled cafes with a drink in one hand and a pen in the other, writing pages of prose about their epiphanies abroad. However, we forget about those who leave with just the money they have in pocket, or those who take on financial burden for the sake of finding out what else lies beyond the confines of the New Jim Crow. [116]

Even when all we find is that anti-blackness knows no borders, some-times leaving is about not being able to breathe. Baldwin said, "All you are ever told in this country about being black is that it is a terrible, terrible thing to be. Now, in order to survive this, you have to really dig down into yourself and recreate yourself, really, according to no image which yet exists...You have to decide who you are, and force the world to deal with you, not with its idea of you."[117] As black people, we carry the burden of the effect of years of blank checks and psychological warfare. We have often allowed such hurt to cloud our vision toward thriving, and we cannot remember or decide if we love or hate this land.

As a black woman, love often comes in the form of revolutionary acts. Journeying to find love of ourselves—our bodies, our hair, the ways we carry ourselves when we silently refuse to walk society's crafted narratives of self-loathing – and then learning to do these things when

---

[116] The "New Jim Crow" refers to the work of Michelle Alexander and others outlining how slavery has been recreated in new systems over the years from sharecropping to Jim Crow to what she calls the New Jim Crow, mass incarceration.

[117] Baldwin, James and Quincy Troupe. *James Baldwin: The Last Interview and Other.*

others watch. Loving the land is no different.

In her essay "Choice," a tribute to Dr. Martin Luther King Jr., Alice Walker recounts the history of dispossession that black people have endured in the U.S. Such dispossession, she writes, leads to people leaving the land of their birth to preserve the good memories they have of it. But for Walker, land belongs to those who have buried their dead there over and over again. While such land is sacred to families, land and space should also belong to those who live it, whose bodies shape its existence and who have been shaped by it as well. Walker thanks Dr. King for the return of the skies and smells of her homeland, and the ability to invite family members to visit and stay, and moreover, stay herself. She wrote that the only ones who had previously stayed were those who could not afford to leave or those too stubborn to be run out.[118] While more people are returning to their roots, to sow seeds they had previously taken elsewhere, there are those who go and return, and go and return, in cycles that allow the passage of air to flow through their lungs more easily.

My mother loves to read, especially about places and their history. She has a list of places she hopes to travel to one day, and when I travel I think about how I am an extension of those dreams. She is always the first I tell about my journeys. I think about her own journey as a mother, and the home she asserted her right to create for herself and her family. In the midst of everything that has tried to claim my power from me, I had the spaces my mother formed to forge an identity of my own creation. It is the type of space and identity that I can carry with me to other lands and other countries.

Blackness abroad is a counter-narrative and a reassertion of the truth that blackness is everywhere. I have often been in circles of other women of colour while we discuss what it has meant and continues to mean for women of colour to make space at places such as Cambridge. To me, however, even more than the importance of existing in spaces

---

[118] Walker, Alice. *In Search Of Our Mothers' Gardens: Womanist Prose*, San Diego: Harcourt Brace Jovanovich, 1983.

that have typically not seen the existence of those like myself, is the ability to choose my own spaces of existence – those created for me to sustain me, where my creativity flourishes without being in direct relation as 'the other,' or forcibly creating an 'other.' Alice Walker spoke of the choice Dr. King gave black people to remain in the South and return home. I revisit choice as this: the ability for home to not be just one space, but rather a myriad of real and imaginary spaces of creation. The types of radical spaces my mother created that allow me to return home. For there is no continuity of place without continuity of the body and mind. It is with those that we make and remake the spaces of our existence. And we cannot have place, we cannot have home, without space. We cannot ask for it, nor can we spend our lives preoccupied with the need for others to acknowledge us and those spaces. We must live them and create them.

There was another moment in Greece, as I was walking along the shoreline of Santorini, that I lifted my arms in the air for a photo, and as I did I looked around me at the vast beauty that was not just the beauty of Santorini, but also what I had exuded as my own Black Girl Magic during my time in Europe. My beauty, wit, style, and boldness of life that had been fully unleashed over the last years felt shockingly at the tips of my fingers. It had always been there. Sometimes it just needed a bit of reminding and revitalising.

I am choosing to create. I am choosing to exist for my own love and my own well-being, and to see that love spill over. I am welcomed home because I have named it so.

Maybe everyone has those path-changing, forming years, and that year was one of mine. It was a year of becoming. The becoming of me, to be exact. It isn't that I had no idea who I was before, or had muddled views and values. In a way, it was a form of unleashing. The unleashing of restraints of years of pent up thoughts, kept locked away in the name of peace and the need to 'wear the mask.' The becoming of an academic who shoves at the walls of academia and moves forward with an ethic of care. The unleashing of the remaining remnants of feeling the need to please others with the decisions I make, even if they hurt me in the process. The becoming of a fresh woman, with the baggage of past relationships slipped off her shoulders and left far behind on a road never to be traversed again. The becoming of a woman capable of taking the clarity and lessons of moments and grasping the complexities of their significance. A woman who found the hands she wanted to hold—especially of other women of colour. The unleashing of a spirit unshakeable enough to go headfirst into storms and reach across divides of space and time to grasp strongly to the things she wants. (Because nothing is as sweet as the things we want most, no matter how hard they are to come by.) It was the year I decided to focus on what it means to dismantle hopelessness.[119]

It was also the year I angered or offended enough people for them to unfollow or unfriend me on social media, to cut off our 'friendship', or to stop inviting me into their circles. The year I was told by varying faces in various places with ferocity and contempt that I was *single, getting old, angry, wrong, a crazy liberal, a radical, a feminist, aggressive, an agitator, a white hater, a reverse racist, privileged, 'too much.'*

In the midst of years of becoming, there are always the voices who try to undo. Some labels are true, and others untrue. It is figuring out the ones to embrace and those to throw aside that's critical to the becoming. It is figuring out that you did not want a seat at the table so much as to remember the lost lesson that your ancestors whispered to you from birth: that to see the table for what it truly is - and what it is made from- means you must also walk away from it. "The path to the wild beyond is paved with refusals." [120]

My mother wrote me a ten-page handwritten letter that I received in the mail about three and a half weeks into my time in Philadelphia. I forget when I am away just how hard returning is. It is not that I do

---

[119] Dismantle hopelessness' is a way I view justice work and a phrase informed by the work of Rev. Michael McBride.
[120] Harney, Stefano. and Fred Moten. *The Undercommons: Fugitive Planning & Black Study,* 2013.

not want to be here, it is just that here and I have held two different courses for so long, that coming back is the meeting of two new worlds. I felt I had gone away to come back to pieces. Shreds of a foreign life. But people move on with or without you, and sometimes they become ghosts or demons. I felt drained and lost, yet on the surface I looked fine. I had more than one night of curling up with my beloved teddy bear pressed tightly against my chest as tears wracked my body, begging God to fill the holes.

I don't think she knows this because I never told her, but my mother's letter saved me in many ways. At night I'd finger the worn edges where loose teardrops had fallen and reread the pages that tethered me to hope. I would reread her story of the long journey that led her to marry my father. I would take solace in the slanted writing talking about how the life she had envisioned for herself was not the one that she eventually found her way to—and how that was okay. She wrote to me about the ways she refutes those who see her as 'just' a stay at home mom. In the end, she wrote words I have now read so often, I have them committed to memory:

"God has done a lot of wonderful things in your life since your birth. It is hard to see it when we perceive those around us getting through in things that we would like to be a part of also. It is easy when we look back and begin to count our successes and blessings. Then we see how overwhelming it is. What we may take for granted another wishes for themselves. You have been chosen for an important part. Nothing great or worthwhile has been easily attained."

When the monachopsis envelops me, hers is the voice of the storyteller, the reminder.

In a year marked by fledgling threads coming undone, I stooped to sew together the pieces into a promise from the words of Warsan Shire:

"My girl is holy, is sacred, is pure
is clean, is loved, is whole, is beautiful
is worthy, is okay, is alone, is just fine
just the way you are girl"[121]

I am imperfectly progressing through life, washed in the perfecting waters of God's grace and delight.

As I stepped deeper into my 20s, returning to the familiar shores of America, I had become the woman I set out to be – even when I did not know she was who I wanted to be. Sometimes angry, and sometimes fearful, but always, always, me. I'm not quite sure what it is that I have figured out. I just know it has been turned on. Perhaps it is the ability to live a bit louder, a little more unapologetically, and a lot more purposefully. While university may have been the space that many of us learned to organise, it isn't where we first gathered knowledge; where we first learned of ourselves and the world.

Over the years, it has been my capacity to love that has buoyed me. A colleague once asked me how I could keep from being consumed by rage with every injustice that goes on around me and to me. I told him that it would be easy to act in accordance to this system of oppression, this world, but it is not the system I wish to uphold; not the world that I want to be part of. I no longer have to remind myself of these truths. I have always lived and grown strong on the fringes. It is my lifeblood.

I often find myself thinking about hands that heal and hands that lift, which come from the encouraging black women who—now and generations before me—affirm my humanity. I have been told that women of colour who write are simply creating 'watered-down' versions of the 'great' writings of white men. But that is just to distract us from our work in ways that we are proving no longer hold power over us. We told these stories before them. We lived and crafted our narratives long before our pens ever hit the paper.

---

[121] Warsan Shire, *"My Girl"*.

Perseverance

Lola Olufemi

We know that political organising requires perseverance. This is true in every space but especially at university, where students juggle their work and organising, where their labour goes unrecognised by the institution. Students carry on organising because they care: because the cause is important, because they understand that feminist and anti-racist work is justice work and therefore a necessity. Organising becomes the means through which they express dissatisfaction, an expression of the need for a more equitable society. In her book, 'Living a Feminist Life' Sara Ahmed provides a framework for willfulness she argues that willful subjects are obstructive; they become the problem because they refuse to ignore the problem. They are persistent, they reoccur, they refuse to be buried. Student organisers are willful subjects. They make themselves deliberately obstructive because they understand that the system should not be allowed to continue in a way that is unjust.

In Cambridge, activism takes many forms. This includes planning direct actions, photo campaigns in JCRs[122], craftivism and the work of the autonomous liberation campaigns who strive to centre the voices of the most marginalised. Students are always finding creative ways to push back against the bounds of an oppressive institution and to think beyond the tradition that it was founded on. This requires perseverance and perseverance can take a toll. Students who organise have asked

---

[122] Junior Combination Room, a acronym for student's main social spaces.

themselves more than once, "How can we exist inside an institution built on structures that are fundamentally oppressive?" "Why organise when we are systematically silenced and erased?" I have asked myself these questions more than once. Why is perseverance important and what does it look like? Why is feminist and anti-racist work necessary?

During an interview at Women of the World Festival in 2017, Black revolutionary Angela Davis argued that challenging hegemonic structures requires an agreement with oneself to wholeheartedly embrace hope. She stressed that this hope is more than just an individual belief in the ability to overcome oppressive structures. It is not about saying "I succeed and so can you" but rather about recognising the power of collective organising. Anti-racist, feminist work is the work of those who understand hope not as an abstract feeling of expectation, but as a foundational belief that another world is possible. It is necessary for the restoration of dignity to oppressed groups, for the redistribution of material resources and for the chance to live full and meaningful lives.

I see perseverance as something deeply tied to this principle. It too, takes many forms. It is a refusal to stop believing, a refusal to become cynical, a refusal to compromise. Perseverance does not have a model. It is at the discretion of the individual who employs it. It does not require us to work ourselves to the bone but instead engage in small acts of resistance on a daily basis. Speaking to friends, sharing an article, informing ourselves about global issues. Regardless of the outcomes of our organising, whether we are alive to see our long or short term goals achieved; the fact that we organise, when others call our aims impossible or unattainable, situates us in a historical legacy of those who have also fought for transformative societies We look to the past to understand the ways that we have succeeded and failed. We do not look to the past for a blueprint for the future, but to understand that the "hope" that Davis mentioned requires a commitment to fighting injustice even when the structures that surround us seem overwhelming and impenetrable.

The origins of this hope are multiple; philosophical, emotional but also rooted in the writings of the present and past. Some organise because it is necessary for their survival. Some organise because they recognise it is necessary for the survival of others. When we organise we rely on the words of those who have challenged the power in a number of different ways across disciplines. They remind us to keep going, to carry on in ways we had not thought possible.

When Lorde tells us that:

The strength of women lies in recognizing differences between us as creative, and in standing to those distortions which we inherited without blame, but which are now ours to alter. The angers of women can transform difference through insight into power. For anger between peers births change, not destruction, and the discomfort and sense of loss it often causes is not fatal, but a sign of growth.[123]

We understand that this means that our feminist movements must be intersectional and constantly evolving. They must not shy away from rage in favour of palatability. Lorde too, hints at the need for perseverance. "The angers of women can transform difference through insight." She is imploring us to keep moving, to carry on recognising our differences as women and non-binary people as the very thing that sustains the feminist movement. We turn back to these words as means of replenishing ourselves and our resistance. We listen.

When Amit Chaudri tells us:

Decolonisation has to do with not only openly discussing the various trans-gressions, and shameful moments and ambitions, that comprise colonial his-tory. It asks for a remedy that will cure us from viewing western history as a history of culture, science, and modernity, and non-western history solely as a history of conflict and race. It would make us hesitate before we situated western politics in a history of constant evolution and redefinition and

---

[123] Audre Lorde, *"The Uses of Anger: Women Responding to Racism"* in Women's Studies Quarterly, Vol. 25. No· 1/2, Looking Back, Moving Forward: 25 Years of Women's Studies History (Spring - Summer, 1997), pp. 277-285.

non-western politics in a history of constant borrowing and reaction.[124]

He situates decolonisation as a process of transforming. He is asking us to flip hegemonic narratives on their head; to think differently about the world that has been presented to us. To fight against the instinct to mythologise the global south and instead locate the multiplicities in its history. *Justice work.*

Drawing from the works of academics and activists in the past and the present shows us that the labor of student activists does not exist in a vacuum. It is not expended without reward. We are adding to the histories we turn back to when we persevere. In the eyes of many, we are hope personified.

---

[124] Amit Chaudri, *"The Real Meaning of Rhodes Must Fall"* in The Guardian, 2016 https://www.theguardian.com/uk.news/2016/mar/16/the-real-meaning-of-rhodes-must-fall

Reflections Upon Three Years

Odelia

What do you say about three years of your life that could summarize the pain, the connections, and the triumphs? I can try to paint a picture through a few words:

Resistance - Every year is marked by tragedies. But in many ways, the post 2016 elections have been a period of hatred and instability in the U.S. like none we have seen in our lifetime. I always knew that Trump could win the election -- I know from my life what that type of hate looks and feels like. it has become exponentially important to check in on others, show up for others, and organise to keep the people around me alive, including myself. Borders are not only at the edges of countries; they are formed in the middle of cities and towns as well.

Pastor Ben McBride had a sermon he gave at my church, The Way Christian Center in Berkeley, where he spoke about how our ancestors who stood behind their slave quarters, mapping their way to freedom, had no way of knowing what would happen to them on the escape. But they must have been driven by the thought that I believe that we will win. I constantly think about all of these ancestors who declared this in their lives, and the blueprints they have left us for collective survival and liberation. I believe that we will win.

For me, resistance has always been in the form of creative resistance. My purpose for this book remains true in my life's work today: to elevate the voices of others around me. It's what I center my work in and what is foundational to the work that I am doing through my most recent venture, Novalia Collective. When I ask myself what world I want to live in and help create, I think about stories and lives free to be who they are, I think about relationships of mutual building and not just mutual survival, and children laughing and playing without fear of death.

Water and deep breaths - I look back on the pieces I wrote for this book, and realise that too much of my life has unjustly consisted of learning more names that I wish I had known before they were attached to a hashtag. Names of people who should still be here like Korryn, Philando, Alton, Stephon. When you realize how many trans women of colour don't return home each night like Celine, Tonya, Keanna. One is always one too many. If I said I have read Danez Smith's "summer, somewhere," a thousand times, it would not be an exaggeration:

> please don't call
> us dead, call us alive someplace better. [1]

My dear friend, sister, and neighbor Amber sends me messages throughout my day reminding me to drink water and to breathe deeply. I want all black people to have that daily reminder. I can get so wrapped up, so consumed, by everything happening in the world that makes it feel like death walks beside me, that I forget the pauses; the simple acts of self-care. Now I leave glasses of water in all the places I frequent.

They are all gone, and nothing about that will ever be fair. But I'm still here, and because I'm here maybe someone else will be able to be here as well. So I remind myself to be gentle to myself, to take deep breaths, and I wake up every morning and read the commitment I wrote to myself on my mirror: *I am a commitment to my heart and the things I need to feel loved, wanted, hopeful, safe, and help me to grow. Those are the things that I let close to my being. And I will not allow the rest to put me out of self.*

---

[1] Smith, Danez. *Don't Call Us Dead: Poems*, 2017.

Faith, joy and love - In an entry from my blog, *Footprints in the Air*, earlier this year, I wrote that I used to mark my years by the tragedies, the pains, but that a few years ago I started to mark them by the promises. When I lean into the moments of joy that those promises have created, it opens me up to more streams of love. I can look back on so many moments of deep, belly-shaking laughter, travels with friends and family, and silences of deep peace. Some of the hardest things have happened in the last three years; things that require a commitment to healing. But joy is abundant and love, infinite. God has done wonders after wonders after wonders. He is always leading me back to myself.

Everything I have written here in this book were truths. I am fiercely proud of the woman I was at Cambridge, and being reminded of that journey has only increased my self-love. And everything I wrote then has also been understood in new ways as I continue to change, to grow, and as God reveals new purpose for my life. I am always becoming. I am especially grateful for my close, writing and creative circles who provide me with the spaces to be challenged: Tabias, Amber, Preston, Moses, Alexandra and Vina.

I continue to look to sunrises to keep going, keep growing, and to keep living. It is a beautiful world when we re-see, re-member and re-make it together.

Suhaiymah

As we complete the final edit of this collection for its publication date in January 2019 I find myself feeling two opposing urges. I am incredibly proud and grateful that this work is being put out into the world. The labours of women of colour are always erased from the annals of history and years from now someone else will try to take credit for the bricks we lay so this book as a testament, record and historic document is essential. But I am also deeply aware of how much I have changed since I wrote it. My essays in this collection are older versions of me. Over the last three years so much has changed both in my personal thinking and life, as well as the world at large. The honesty of my works as they are in this book are an honesty about growth and vulnerability. I want these essays to be read in the way I wrote them because people can easily access my more recent writings on Islamophobia, feminism, decoloniality, knowledge production and more at my blog and online – but the thinking I did to get here deserves acknowledgement too, we are all always growing.

My little sister started university this year and her experiences have reminded me, for the first time in three years, of the daily visceral difficulty that being a Muslim woman of colour in higher education is. Her experiences have also encouraged me not to edit my twenty-year-old self. I believe that my younger-self's voice will be a better companion to those who need it than my current voice. I can write a book critiquing the structures and histories of interconnected violence in the world any time – I can research and refine it – but I can never recreate the set of moments, crucial relationships and thousands of experiences that made this specific iteration of this book possible. It is this version of my essays that I want in the world because it is this version of myself that I would want my eighteen-year-old self to hear from. It may be selfish but my essays are, above all, for her and anyone like her.

Reading over the poems in this book is interesting because at the time of initial writing I couldn't have anticipated that poetry would become something so central in my life or so crucial a vessel for the sharing of my truths as it is today. Another thing that intrigues me in my own writing is the place of Allah. I am both mildly disappointed and pleasantly grateful that Allah is much more central to my existence now than perhaps during my time at Cambridge.

That is not to say that submission to God's will – Islam – was not central to my university experience. In fact, the isolation, oppression and alienation I experienced at times brought me closer to Allah than I ever had been before Cambridge. But even in my desire for liberation, justice and decolonised forms of knowledge at university, I underprivileged the word of Allah itself. Nonetheless, I am not ashamed to share that version of myself as I believe we need more vulnerability and honesty around discussing our relationships with God, our changes of heart, and our growth as people. Today I am much more comfortable and aware of centring the worship of Allah in my life and maintaining that as the key motive behind all I do and all I will be accountable for – if Allah wills.

The general gist of what I have written herein is the general gist of what I still believe. My experience at Cambridge irrefutably radicalised me but my critiques have also matured. Since graduating I have completed a master's degree in Postcolonial Studies where I focused on gender and queer theory to write about how the British state surveils and polices Muslims through the way it imagines our gender and sexualities. After completing that I somewhat shunned academia and travelled the country – as well as internationally – performing poetry, giving talks and educational workshops. I have met hundreds of people and shared difficult, daunting and delicate conversations over the past two years. I have had these conversations in spaces ranging from mosques, to student unions, to LGBTQ poetry nights, to women's marches, to schools, to Islamic society events, to music festivals. Allah has blessed me with the ability to meet and reach such a range of people and those experiences have changed me.

If I were to write this book today I would focus more explicitly on Islamophobia. I would discuss Prevent[2] and the way it affects Muslim students due to the British state's 'counter-radicalisation' strategy. This strategy views all Muslims as inherently predisposed to violence, thus legitimising surveilling us, policing us and violating our human rights. I would write less about being 'brown' – a term I don't find particularly useful these days - and more about disrupting narratives than disproving stereotypes. I would discuss feminism with more complication due to the way it has been weaponised against Muslims and co-opted by Islamophobia as well as institutions like the violent border regime – topics I have written about much in the years since writing these essays. I would also probably write less romantically about Pakistan from a cringe-inducing diaspora point of view.

The world is much more complicated than I sometimes drew it out to be when I was nineteen and twenty. My preoccupations now are revealing state violence and creating holistic communities of healing which centre understanding violence as a political and social issue linked to capitalism, history, racism and more. In that sense I am very much still invested in 'decolonising' our histories, ways of knowing and understandings of each other and to me that now means I am invested in contextualising people; searching out the excluded and erased; and

---

[2] Prevent is short for 'Preventing Violent Extremism', part of the British government's counter-terrorism strategy. It rests on the notion that violent extremism can be prevented by intervening in 'non-violent extremism' which is allegedly possible to spot through "signs" such as increased religiosity and changed appearance (the science behind this has been criticised even by those who themselves undertook it). This legitimises the policing of ideologies, traits and behaviours deemed problematic by the state because they can be deemed precursors to violence or crime being committed.

challenging myself to divest from the circumstances I benefit from that see others harmed.

Several years after studying at Cambridge it is sometimes hard to remember how *difficult* it was. Subsequently this book is a reminder of what I, and three of the women I most leaned on, experienced. I am very proud of this work, alhamdulilah. Above all, the fact it now exists means that a nineteen-year-old girl somewhere feeling alone can hold it, read it, and feel understood. If this book does that then it has done everything I ever needed it to do.

Waithera

My first experience of the hostile environment came when I was 15-years-old as I watched my mother and sister struggle to navigate the suddenly byzantine student visa rules introduced under then Home Secretary, Theresa May. I described the rising costs of visas that year to an English friend as we stood in a school corridor waiting for our Spanish teacher to arrive, and lamented the lack of accountability surrounding decision-making on approvals and denials. Jokingly, I concluded that Theresa May must really not like immigrants. With a look of indignation he told me that I was being racist and ignored me for the rest of the lesson. Today, he would wholeheartedly agree with me.

I'm quick to acknowledge that struggling to get an expensive student visa in this country is a very middle-class problem. But it acted as a gateway to me wanting to understand the harrowing experience of asylum seekers and less well-off immigrants, not just in the UK but across the Western world. My journey through and outside of this book has been characterised by the realisation that my struggle constitutes the easiest state of black immigrants in this country, and yet it still evidences white supremacist ideology in government policy.

All of our writing provides a snapshot of life before Brexit or Trump. What is often attributed to an ostensibly brand-new "rise of the right" can be seen very clearly to have existed in various forms since the first European settler colonialist set foot on land that wasn't his centuries ago. Not only is nothing that we're currently seeing new, people of colour have been trying to point out that it exists for years. And we have been shunned as race-baiters, people with chips on their shoulders, reverse racists, and the PC police.

What is new for me is that I have stopped trying to fight against these labels. My time with FLY and as CUSU Women's Officer sparked a new goal in me to help empower other women (particularly WoC) to understand that their experiences are political and fight accordingly. I no longer feel guilty when someone entitled (white or male or both) calls me "snowflake" for being unwilling to engage their bad faith arguments.

I recall an experience educating a then conservative-leaning friend on cultural appropriation shortly after this manuscript had been completed. During term-time, I wrote her a heavily-referenced 2,000 word essay explaining why cultural appropriation was an issue deserving of our attention. She read it, accepted finally that it was an issue, but concluded that she had no interest in tackling it. I realised then that there are two immense steps to be taken in convincing those for whom the rights and interests of black women are simply an interesting debate to actually fight on our side. First, we must endure their devil's advocacy, as if the devil cannot advocate for himself. And next, if we can convince them that our ideals are worth considering, we must convince them that those ideals are also worth fighting for. It is a battle I am no longer willing to take up without (extremely) good reason.

Beyond my interactions with majority groups, I have deepened my knowledge of solidarity politics. Reading Audre Lorde's accounts of solidarity with black women living in apartheid South Africa in "A Burst of Light" made me particularly ashamed that my support for Palestinians in their own efforts for freedom have been so superficial. I now turn my gaze not just to BLM organisers in the US but to ethnic, religious, and cultural minorities globally who are reaching out their hands for ours.

I have heard every critique of identity politics – some good, most in bad faith – and appreciated that I owe my teenage knowledge of the hostile environment to it. Immigrants in this country could have written essays on it long before Amelia Gentleman used her position to thrust the problem into the spotlight.

For me, much of the value of this book is to stress that point. Not a petty I-told-you-so but an urge to you, the reader, to listen. To set aside your gut instinct that this country is fair and good and wonder why the pesky minorities you might quietly resent have been banging on about the same issue for decades. Consider that your position might be blinding you to truths that, if left to unravel, will leave your descendants mumbling new platitudes about "never again".

Writing and publishing this book has been an honour. I have been carried by the superior intellect and writing ability of my co-authors, who continue to inspire me, and to whom I owe a massive debt. I still have a lot to learn but I hope my words contribute in a small way to someone else's radical awakening. I hope my chapters act as a genuine guide.

Lola

Many of my contributions to this collection were written in my first or second year at Cambridge, (the last chapter contains more recent reflections) These articles were responses to frustrations, racist and sexist microaggressions and alienations that at the time felt urgent to articulate in the face of overwhelming silence. I used the FLY Blog and student newspapers to ask questions of myself, my peers and the institution and found solidarity in doing so. My writing was integral to the organising work I did as a student. I wrote down my thoughts and experiences in an attempt to try and understand them a little better. My knowledge, theoretical framework, priorities and ability to articulate myself have grown since then but in these essays, I see the beginnings of a criticality that the feminist and anti-racist organising spaces in Cambridge helped me to hone. I include lightly edited versions of these essays here because I understand the importance of political education. I include them with the hope that they resonate with someone, somewhere and open the door to crafting a radical framework that extends far beyond reflecting on our experiences in elite institutions.

Context matters. It goes without saying that if this book were written in the present moment, it would be different. But this collection is a process of thinking out loud and will hopefully allow readers to trace the routes through which we came to our political understandings.

"Words have their own firmness. The word on the page may not reveal (may conceal) the flabbiness of the mind that conceived it. >
All thoughts are upgrades — get more clarity, definition, authority,

by being in print - that is, detached from the person who thinks them.
A potential fraud — at least potential — in all writing." [3]
- Susan Sontag

---

[3] An extract from the Diaries of Susan Sontag.

GLOSSARY

Cisgender – denoting or relating to a person whose sense of personal identity and gender corresponds with their birth sex.

Paki – a derogatory racial slur used in reference to South Asian migrants in Britain from around the 1960s. Whilst an abbreviation of "Pakistani" its usage is typically irrespective of national background as it is a racist label for anyone of South Asian heritage.

Comprehensive school – a secondary school that is state funded and therefore doesn't select its intake on the basis of academic achievement – e.g. not selective.

Tripos – the name for the undergraduate examinations at Cambridge university.

Access Officer – a student position on a college's student governing body that is responsible for and working towards widening participation work (often in collaboration with a college employee working on the same).

Porters – members of college staff who work on-site and often manage who comes in and out of college entrances.

Orientalist – the representation and discussion of asia/south asia and the middle east in a way typified by colonial attitudes and racist logics.

Reverse Racism - The idea that racism goes both ways and that it is possible to be 'racist' as opposed to prejudiced against white people.

White Gaze - The centering of whiteness and the ever-present preoccupation of whiteness with non-white lives.

Epistemology – referring to the theory of knowledge: what we know, how we know it and what we count as 'knowing' and 'knowledge' - especially with regard to its methods, validity, and scope, and the distinction between justified belief and opinion.

Gaslighting - a form of psychological manipulation that sows doubt in the targeted individual or members of a targeted group, making them question their own memory, perception of reality, and sanity.

Misogynoir - Misogyny (contempt for women) directed towards black women where race and gender both play roles in bias. It was coined by queer black feminist Moya Bailey, who created the term to address misogyny directed toward black women in American visual and popular culture.

ACKNOWLEDGEMENTS

Our gratitude and love go to the following:

Suhaiymah –
The endlessly inspiring friends who co-authored this book with me, it is a genuine honour to share these pages with you. A special thanks to Odelia for coming up with the beautiful idea for this book and for taking the helm with it. To the women who founded FLY, it would not be an exaggeration to say it changed my life. To everyone who flocks to it weekly just to hold each other up. To the people who shed tears with me and gave me space to work things through. To my grandparents for parting with everything they knew, and finally, always, to my mother for everything that I cannot put into words but that I hope she knows she has done for me. My ultimate thanks go to Allah – may I have the ability to be truly grateful.

Odelia –
My powerful co-authors who I break bread with through language within these pages. FLY for bringing us together at a time that I needed to know that the depths of isolation are never felt alone. Alexandra Wilcox, DJ Smolinsky, Shelly Knight Ernst, Jordan Younge and everyone else who constantly supported and encouraged me, and gave me feedback to finish this work. My mother, whose lifelong love of exploring the world through writing has forever impacted my own life. My family, for teaching me to reflect and love from afar. And to God, for all that He has provided and will provide as my faith teaches me how to walk this land.

Waithera –
To the women who co-authored this book and Odelia for her leadership. To the founders of FLY and its current and future members. And to all the women who gifted me with a black feminist ethic.

Lola –
To every single person who turned up to a FLY meeting and shared a part of themselves, thank you. To my co-authors, the founders of FLY and the CUSU Women's Campaign – who shaped my politics in ways I cannot begin to describe.

ABOUT VERVE POETRY PRESS

Verve Poetry Press is a new press focussing initially on meeting a local need in Birmingham - the need for the vibrant poetry scene here in Brum to find a way to present itself to the poetry world via publication. Co-founded by Stuart Bartholomew and Amerah Saleh, it published poets in its first year from all corners of the city - poets that represent the city's varied and energetic qualities and are able to communicate its many poetic stories.

As well as publishing wonderful collections from poets with local links, such as Casey Bailey, Nafeesa Hamid, Leon Priestnall, Rupinder Kaur and Polarbear, we have also been working with other poets who have close connections to our sister festival, Verve. Our Experimental Pamphlet Series, our poetry show collection from Matt Abbott and our anthology in aid of CALM on the subject of male suicide all fall on this side of our activity. Like the festival, we strive to think about poetry in inclusive ways and embrace the multiplicity of approaches towards this glorious art.

This important book - part poetry, part memoir, part essay - marks a departure for us into the world of Non-Fiction and prose. But it continues our tradition of publishing work of quality that needs in our view to see print, but which has been overlooked for all sorts of reasons. We are thrilled to have been able to help bring it to you now.

We have an exciting time ahead. Best keep your eye on us!

www.vervepoetrypress.com
@VervePoetryPres
mail@vervepoetrypress.com